Tuning In To Grace

CISTERCIAN STUDIES SERIES:
NUMBER ONE HUNDRED TWENTY-NINE

Tuning In To Grace

The Quest for God

ANDRÉ LOUF

Translated by
John Vriend

CISTERCIAN PUBLICATIONS
Kalamazoo, Michigan — Spencer, Massachusetts

First published in the United States in 1992 by
Cistercian Publications Inc.
WMU Station
Kalamazoo, Michigan 49008

Translation © 1992 Cistercian Publications

First published in Dutch as *Inspelen op Genade*
© 1984 Uitgeverij Lannoo, Tielt

The work of Cistercian Publications is made possible in part
by support from Western Michigan University to the
Institute of Cistercian Studies.

Phototypeset by Intype, London
Printed in the United States of America

CONTENTS

Preface   vii

1 Continuing in One's Conversion   1
    Between wrath and grace   1
    Always a convert   5
    The hardened righteous   7

2 Our Idols and God   12
    The unfaithful people   12
    Idols for today   16
    To curse God   18
    A hearsay God   26

3 The Power of Faith   28
    How shall we speak of faith?   28
    The astonishment of Jesus   30
    Endorsement and self-surrender   33
    A miracle-working faith   34

4 Growing by Being Tested   38
    The weakness of the flesh   38
    God's power manifest in weakness   42
    Being reconciled with one's weakness   45

5 Between Weakness and Grace   48
    Evangelical virtue?   48
    Pharisee or publican?   52
    The Good News   56

6 Contrition of the Heart 59
  Guilt and repentance 61
  The monk and the publican 64
  Ascesis? 66
  The ascesis of weakness 70
  The restored human being 75

7 Spiritual Companionship 78
  Getting in touch with 'life' 80
  Like the Father 82
  Uncovering one's desires 88
  Internal censorship 91
  The mirror image 96
  The true God for the free person 99
  Key aspects of companionship 102

8 On Some of the Fruits of the Spirit 109
  Joy 109
  Turning inward and being silent 118
  To grow inwardly 121
  A humble love 124

9 Growing in Grace through Prayer 129
  A word on prayer 129
  Prayer in weakness 132
  Prayer as a cry 137
  Integration from the inside out 142
  Freedom in the Spirit 144

Postscript 146

PREFACE

IN THIS BOOK I have brought together texts that were composed in very diverse circumstances. Most of them owe their existence to talks given at conferences and copied from tape recordings, some of which were then published as articles.

In putting the book together I was struck by the fact that most of these texts basically attempt to give voice to the same experience, although each from a different perspective. The topic each time is our life with God: how to enter into contact with him, how to become more aware of him, how to grow in his grace and Spirit. These are the themes in which, in recent years and rather unexpectedly, a great deal of interest has surfaced. God has again risen, splendidly alive, from the death to which, barely thirty years ago, most people assigned him. Everywhere people are going out in search of the religious, the spiritual, and this – no doubt in all sincerity – in all directions.

About such spiritual experience this book makes no new or startling claims. It seeks to be no more than an attempt to describe and illumine some of the most fundamental experiences that are part of an evangelical quest for God, experiences no believer can skip if he or she wants to get closer to God.

These experiences are rarely immediately clear. For most of us it takes a fairly long time before we can understand them and accept them as actual experiences in our lives. We are indeed in search of God but have a hard time finding the correct wavelength. We do indeed pray for grace but it is difficult for us to position ourselves in that place where alone grace can come to us. Often we are bravely at work but not always on the right way, the road where God has so long been waiting for us.

Hence the title: *Tuning in to Grace*. Is not that the only question of importance to the God-seeker? How we can attune ourselves to grace? It always takes a lifetime to do – and this because God wants it so. It is certainly not the intention of this book, therefore, to point the reader to a short cut that is quicker. As we know, it does not exist. Our hope is only that these pages may serve to make clearer to some readers what is actually going on when for years they have to grope their way in dark faith and blind love, seemingly so miserable and with no sign of success. And how intensely God is nevertheless at work in their lives – with a patience as great as his love!

ANDRÉ LOUF

1

CONTINUING IN ONE'S CONVERSION

Between wrath and grace

WHEN THE SURPRISE of grace comes over someone for the first time, we speak of 'conversion'.* The person is then assumed to be in the process of being converted or of converting. In ordinary usage these words refer to a very important but nevertheless passing event. It may still be to come, or perhaps it happened long ago, but no one seems to think it might have to be repeated – barring, of course, a radical disowning of the faith. Accordingly, the concept 'convert', which derives from 'conversion', only concerns a clearly defined category of believers: those who were not confronted with the faith until adult life. From this it follows that those who were baptized in infancy and so imbibed the faith from childhood, and that describes the majority of us, will never be called converts and conversion would never in any sense seem applicable to them. Only those who live outside the faith, or those who do not live by their faith (and hence are caught in sin) could experience conversion – not the ordinary, and certainly not the devout, believer.

Against this it must be stated, however, that the Bible expressly and constantly speaks about repentance or conversion as something that concerns everyone. The very first announcement of the Good News, which comes to us from the lips of John the Baptist, is this crisp summons: 'Repent,

*The Dutch word *bekering*, which I translated as 'conversion', denotes both repentance and conversion. Since the author clearly has in mind the broader concept, I have opted for the latter. But see also the note on p. 5. *Translator.*

for the kingdom of Heaven is at hand' (Matt. 3:1). It is this being 'at hand' which so powerfully necessitates conversion. For, said John to the Pharisees and Sadducees who came to him to be baptized, the wrath and vengeance of God are at hand:

> You brood of vipers! Who warned you to flee from the coming wrath? Produce good fruit as evidence of your repentance . . . Even now the axe lies at the root of the trees. Therefore every tree that does not bear good fruit will be cut down and thrown into the fire. I am baptizing you with water, for repentance, but the one who is coming after me is mightier than I. I am not worthy to carry his sandals. He will baptize you with the holy Spirit and fire. His winnowing fan is in his hand. He will clear his threshing floor and gather his wheat into his barn, but the chaff he will burn with unquenchable fire.   (Matt. 3:7–12)

John the Baptist connected repentance with Jesus, but at the same time with the coming judgement, the sudden outbreak of the wrath of God from which we urgently need to be rescued. To us wrath and vengeance, when attributed to God, are not self-evident concepts, any more than is the figure of the axe which is said to lie at our roots. Consciously or unconsciously we have relegated this notion to the Old Testament, as though with the coming of Jesus it totally disappeared from the horizon and became completely obsolete. But here, at the very threshold of the New Testament, the coming of Jesus is announced with the aid of this ancient and still common imagery. In the person of Jesus, God took his winnowing fan in hand and was at the point of cleansing his threshing floor. This is what has to happen to us in the baptism that Jesus brings, a baptism for repentance but also of fire and the Holy Spirit. This seems to show that at some point we have to be confronted with the wrath of God, but at the same time that this can happen only in Jesus. Have I already encountered the wrath of God in my life? And if not, do I still need grace? Does grace not always point to the wrath from which I am rescued every moment? In Jesus, am I not continually exposed to the wrath and to the grace of God, somewhere at a point between wrath and grace, an in-between point that could perhaps be conversion?

Also, at a time when Jesus had long been dead and raised up, Paul would still, in the opening section of his great theological synthesis on grace, write to the Romans: 'The wrath of God is being revealed' (Rom. 1:18). Admittedly, in another passage Paul was to announce that the glory of God is also being disclosed to us (Rom. 8:18); still, wrath here precedes glory. For 'by nature,' says Paul again, 'we were children of wrath' (cf. Eph. 2:3). Love and grace, then, are an exception to the wrath that is being revealed and presuppose that in a special way we were chosen to be rescued from it. The state of grace is an exception to the state of wrath, which is really our state at birth; hence it is a most loving exception which we owe to Jesus Christ, the Son of God.

In several passages of the New Testament we learn more about the wrath of God, namely, that actually it is not yet past but still to come. Rather than being past, it awaits us in the future. Quite often Paul uses the expression 'the wrath is coming' (Eph. 5:6; Col. 3:6), whereas John prefers to speak of the wrath which has already come but remains upon us (John 3:36). The Apocalypse looks for the 'great day of wrath', the day on which God will give to the nations 'the cup of the fury of his wrath' to drink (Rev. 16:19).

The image of the cup of his wrath, which God has to give us to drink, comes very close to that other cup of which Scripture speaks: the cup of Jesus' suffering. In the hands of Jesus the cup of wrath became the cup of salvation; the deadly drink of fury became the drink of love. Like Jesus, we in turn will come to drink of that cup from the hands of God. And for us also that cup is either the cup of wrath or the cup of love, and we will either become intoxicated with God's fury or drunk with his love. The latter can happen to us only together with Jesus and thanks to Jesus. For that reason our cup of suffering can be no other than that of Jesus himself. He alone, because in his love he emptied that cup to the very dregs, can save us from the wrath of God, ensuring that the cup of wrath will also be for us the cup of salvation.

All this is far from being accomplished and is not altogether assured, though Paul exhorts us to look forward to the coming wrath with confidence:

> For God proves his love for us in that while we were still sinners Christ died for us. How much more then, since we are now justified by his blood, will we be saved through him from the wrath. Indeed, if, while we were enemies, we were reconciled to God through the death of his Son, how much more, once reconciled, will we be saved by his life. (Rom. 5:8–10)

Elsewhere Paul adds that it is Jesus who 'delivers us from the coming wrath' (1 Thess. 1:10). Hence, we were saved from wrath a first time when our sins were forgiven in baptism. But we will be confronted a second time with the same wrath of God, and this remains a continuing possibility in the future. For that reason the present, today, is so important. Today is the *kairos*, the time of salvation in which we now live and in which it is already given to us, in the power and resurrection of Jesus, to make the decisive choice. For that which comes tomorrow is already given today, though only in anticipation and in progress toward ultimate completion.

That decisive choice, the choice of tomorrow and already today, and of today for tomorrow, between wrath and grace, is precisely what we call 'repentance'. This word is the English translation of the New Testament word *metanoein*, which in turn is an attempt at rendering the Hebrew *shûb*. This Semitic stem simply means 'to turn about', 'to retrace one's steps' and, only in a derivative sense, 'to repent'. Hence in this word the accent lies on the turn-about which occurs in such a process. Now, the Greek word *metanoein* clearly illumines the nature of that turn-about. Present in it are two stems of which the first, as in the Hebrew, underscores the turn-about; upside-down, or about-face. The second stem teaches us what it is precisely that is subject to such a reversal: the nous, i.e. our spiritual centre, the deepest dimension of our heart. At stake, then, is a reversal in our interior self. Sometimes *metanoein* is translated as 'penitence', but that seems less apt than 'repentance'. But the word 'repentance', especially in the commonly used sense, is really still too weak. Elsewhere, in a similar context, the Bible speaks of *metanoein kai epistrephein* (Acts 3:19), to make a total about turn in order to turn to something or someone. Involved, then, is a radical conversion by which a person retraces his or her steps and strikes out in a new direction.*

Always a convert

Here again we face the question with which we started this chapter: in what sense do we still need repentance or conversion today? Did we not receive it along with our baptism, once and for all? Our conversion is behind us and now we are on the way – admittedly with ups and downs, with stumblings and risings – to perfection and holiness. That indeed is the unconscious image we carry with us of the road on which all Christians travel. This road, roughly speaking, is divided into three stages: first, unbelief or sin; then the decisive step of conversion; and finally, the pursuit of perfection. We spontaneously, and rather naively, tend to place ourselves somewhere in that third stage, at a more or less advanced level.

Reality, however, is not so simple. Not that it is complicated; grace is simplicity itself. To state it more precisely, life in the holy Spirit is not easy to discern. Different power lines continually cross each other so that – because it is not always clear how to tell them apart – confusion, even illusion, remains a possibility. For sin, repentance and grace cannot simply be divided into three stages. In ordinary experience they are often inextricably bound up together. They grow together and interact with each other. I am never one hundred per cent one or the other; I am continually all three at once. Sin, repentance and grace are my daily life and lot. Also in the kingdom of heaven, to the extent that we live it in the world today, that is how it is, says Jesus. There, too, you find

---

The New Jerusalem Bible has a helpful note under Matthew 3: '*Metanoia* or change of heart means a renunciation of sin, repentance. This regret for past conduct is normally accompanied by a "conversion" by which a person turns back to God and enters upon a new life. The words used for these two complementary aspects of the same movement of heart are often the same, see Acts 2:38; 3:19.' *Translator.*

easier to wake from a dream than the dream of a saint. — Osho

sinners; in fact, tax collectors and prostitutes precede others there (Matt. 21:28–32).

These three dimensions assume neither a hierarchy nor a scale of values. We do not go from one to another, as on the steps of a ladder. They are not stripes or ribbons we may successively sew on our sleeves. On the contrary, until death we never completely say farewell to any one of these three. We constantly remain sinners and remain unremittingly caught up in conversion, and in this process we are continually being sanctified by the Spirit of God. We can never belong to the class of people of whom Jesus said that they 'have no need of repentance' (Luke 15:7) because they thought of themselves as righteous (Luke 18:9). For then we would have no need of Jesus. We would then be capable of going it alone on our journey Godward, alone in the most dreadful sense of the word, of being *all alone*, ever and again falling back on ourselves and on the appearance of a sanctity we would attempt to produce out of our own resources. And so we would constantly grow more deeply frustrated because real love would always elude us.

It is always an illusion to think that one has been converted once and for all. The truth is we are always merely sinners, forgiven sinners, that is, sinners-in-a-state-of-forgiveness, sinners-in-the-process-of-conversion. On earth there can be no other holiness, because grace does not relate to us in any other way. To repent is ever and again to take our place in this inner reversal: the turning of our human finiteness – Paul calls it 'flesh' – toward the grace of God. It is a turning from the law of the letter to the law of the Spirit and of freedom, from wrath to grace. This reversal is never finished, because the truth is that it has always only just started. Anthony the Great, the well known patriarch and father of all monks, said it pithily: 'Every morning again I say to myself, today I start.' And Abba Poimen, after Anthony the second most famous of the ancient fathers, when on his death-bed people congratulated him because after a blessed and virtuous life he was permitted to go out to meet God in full confidence, replied: 'I am still a beginner; I had barely started with my conversion.' And as he said this, he wept.

Accordingly, conversion always has something to do with

time. A human being needs time, and God wants to take time with us. We would be assuming a completely false image of humanity should we suppose that the important things in human life can take place at once, or once for all. Human beings are so created that they need time to grow, to mature, to develop their full potential. God knows this much better than we do. For that reason he waits, he does not stop caring, he is long-suffering and patient. A Dutch poet once wrote that God waits for us like a patient fisherman. *To chrèston tou Theou eis metanoian se agei*, 'The kindness of God leads you to repentance,' wrote Paul (Rom. 2:4). Not in the first place his wrath, but on the contrary *to chrèston*, his generosity, goodness, patience. In the prologue to his Rule, Benedict offered a striking commentary on this kindness. Every day God is looking expectantly toward his servant, said Benedict, and the time he still measures out to us is *ad inducias*, a respite, an extra allowance, a time of grace we receive into the bargain, a period we may use to meet God still another time, and to meet him ever better in his marvellous mercy. Not until later, after our death, will we also live timelessly in the once-for-all. Now, however, time is there as an opportunity to better our own knowledge of God. It is always a time of repentance and grace, a gift of God's mercy.

The hardened righteous

So every day God works with us, calling us to repentance: 'Oh that today you would hear his voice: "Harden not your hearts . . ."' (Ps. 95:7-8). God speaks in various ways. He speaks through his Word, through the people with whom we live, through all sorts of circumstances, joyful and painful. We dread the latter especially. We know all too well that God has something to say to us in affliction, sickness, death or misfortune. If we still sense this fear in our heart, it is because as yet we have eyes only for the wrath of God, and this means we have not yet discovered how, behind the external signs of wrath, his immeasurable love is concealed. As we saw before, in Jesus the wrath of God turned into love. Or, rather, it has become clear that his wrath is nothing other than an initial, provisional attempt to make us understand his love.

If we are still afraid of God's intervention, if we still spontaneously interpret this intervention as an expression of his wrath, this means that somehow we have got stuck in this expression of the provisional. We have not yet had the opportunity to run squarely into the love of God, to be thrown upside down by his tenderness. Perhaps someone will reply that in fact this fear is proof that at some point we *are* guilty, that our conscience is accusing us, that we *do* deserve to be punished by God. Only sinners need to be afraid of God's wrath, and anyone who is afraid thereby proves that he or she belongs to the category of sinners. But, though this is likely to be the reaction of the average believer of today, it is not self-evident. After all, even a superficial glance at the gospel would suggest that perhaps sinners do not need to be afraid of Jesus. Was there not a frequent charge against him that he preferred to spend time with sinners, and did he not consistently answer this charge by saying that he came not for the righteous but for sinners? (Matt. 9:13).

Also it has not at all been proved that only sinners are afraid of God. One also encounters many devout believers, many 'righteous' (to use a biblical term) who are just as unsure and fearful in awaiting a possible encounter with God. Accordingly, they do their utmost to ward off this uneasiness with the aid of a strong dose of virtuousness. The more they succeed – and such success is always very relative – the better chance they have, or so they think, of escaping the wrath of God and of earning his love.

Indeed, there are two kinds of people who, for the present, will still have to 'settle accounts' with the wrath of God. They are the hardened sinners and the hardened righteous. The hardened sinner, who wants nothing to do with any kind of turn-about, will in the end have to fear the wrath of God, even though he cleverly manages to hide his fear in daily life. I would be inclined to think, however, that in actual fact only a very small number of hardened sinners exist.

There are, I think, many more 'hardened righteous', in a manner of speaking, who have no more knowledge than hardened sinners of God's measureless mercy, and who steadfastly attempt to do more good only because they are afraid of God's wrath. Admittedly, for short periods they may be able to free themselves from that fear, to the extent that they succeed in realizing a part of their ideal self-image in daily life. In the long run things may even be bearable, but actually they live on a very meagre diet of comfort. For that reason they are seldom convincing and even less 'infectious'. For they still know nothing of love, and what is alive in them is rooted in a kind of self-sufficiency and self-absorption which tend to isolate them even further from others. As Jesus himself said: 'They have received their reward' (Matt. 6:2), and because they know nothing of grace they do not yearn for anything else. Their life would be without prospect were it not that the expression 'hardened' (which we applied both to certain sinners and to certain righteous folk) is in fact basically wrong in that it suggests a definite status. For, on the contrary, everything is provisional; that is to say, both hardened sinners and the hardened righteous exist equally in time, a time God has granted both as a time of grace and thus a time for repentance. There is neither hardened sinner nor hardened righteous, but only a sinner who may continually be caught up in a conversion process.

This is what I should like to make clear in the course of this book from a variety of viewpoints. It is certainly not immediately obvious, nor is it easy to explain; one cannot crystallize it in a definition. One can only attempt to describe it from within the perspective of limited personal experience and from that of the experience of others one may have met. It is actually easier to define what it is not, because in fact it is much 'cheaper' to live as a hardened sinner or a hardened righteous person than as a sinner-in-process-of-conversion. And yet, it is this internal reversal at which grace is always aiming, day in and day out. For it is God who comes to touch us in countless ways to teach us conversion. We can only hold ourselves in readiness to let ourselves be disturbed and emotionally moved by God. For a great deal has to happen that lies outside the reach of our good will and our natural generosity. Reversal means, not merely that we will be inwardly wounded, but that we must be shaken to our very foundations. It means that perhaps we will be broken, that something inside us will collapse – something like a concrete bunker on which we worked perhaps for years with exemplary

care but which at a given moment began to function solely
as a defence system against our deepest self, against others,
with the risk that in the end it would protect us even against
God's grace.

That collapse is only just the beginning, even though a
hopeful one. We must be on our guard not to try to build up
again what grace has broken down. This is something we
have to learn, for there is always a strong temptation to put
scaffolding up around that crumbling facade and to tidy it
up. We must learn to acquiesce in the collapse and to sit
down amid the rubble without bitterness or self-reproach –
also without reproaching God – but with hopeful resignation,
full of surrender, confident as a child who dreams that his
father will fix things again, that he knows how to rebuild
them, in a very different way now but much better than
before. We must be like the prodigal son, so much of whose
life lay in ruins: his credit, his honour, his human heart; he
had lost everything he could expect from earthly sources and
nevertheless made the decision to go back to his father with
confidence, sensing intuitively that behind the servant role,
which he was ready to adopt, he might be allowed to become
again the son. Once a son, always a son. The very same
moment he was reconciled with the wreckage of his life, he
was at home with his father. But someone who is still fighting
his own wreckage is still at war with his Father and his God,
is still wide open to the wrath of God and still unable to
acknowledge the love. But they who give themselves up to the
point of being content and are able to accept their own misery
have already abandoned themselves to redeeming love.

This way of continuing in the conversion process is something we can do only for Jesus' sake, as we are sent on our
way and empowered by the Spirit of God. We will then
experience what happened long ago with Jesus in the mystery
of his death and resurrection. Jesus' trust in, and surrender
to, his Father through death have forever taken the sting out of
God's wrath and enable us, together with Jesus, to recognize
through every death and mortification the Father's love, even
in our own deepest weakness. *That* is conversion, a continual
switching over to sin and grace. Please note that I do not
mean *from* sin *to* grace, but switching over to sin *and* grace.

This means to let go of self-justification and of our own righteousness, to acknowledge our sin and to open ourselves to the grace of God.

This is the miracle of the sinner who continues in the conversion process, whom Jesus himself acknowledged to be the one who furnishes the greatest joy to the Father in heaven: 'I tell you, in just the same way there will be more joy in heaven over one sinner who repents than over ninety-nine righteous people who have no need of repentance' (Luke 15:7). Such a person is the joy and pride of the Father, the amazing Easter-person who continually dies in Jesus and rises with him. It is a daily miracle, never completed, because God has never finished it before our time here below has run out. Our time and the duration of our life are also forms of incarnate grace, God's love crystallized into a time-span. Thus each day we may gratefully remain on the path of conversion. To take a single step outside that path would be to take a step outside God and his love, even though we still think of God, speak about God, proclaim God. Only to pray to God would from that time be impossible, for there is no genuine prayer outside continual conversion.

Outside conversion we stand outside Love, leaving us only two possibilities – either self-sufficiency and self-righteousness, or profound discontent and despair.

We cannot stand before God in any way other than in the conversion process, for otherwise we would end up not with God but with one of many idols. Nor can we continue in the conversion process outside God, for repentance is never the fruit of good intentions or attentive effort. It is the first step of love, God's love more than ours. Repentance is our yielding to God's urgent intervention, our surrender to the first signs of love we sense coming from him. It is surrender in the strong sense of capitulation. We capitulate; we are allowed to give up before God. All our defences melt away before the consuming fire of his Word and glance. All that remains to us, then, is the prayer of Jeremiah the prophet: 'Make us come back to you, Yahweh, and we will come back.' (Lam. 5:21 JB)

2

OUR IDOLS AND GOD

What about silence?

CONTINUING IN CONVERSION is the only way a person can come finally to the one true God, the God of Jesus Christ. If we fail to meet this condition we actually still belong at home with our idols and can say little or nothing about God. The apostle John, putting the finishing touches to his first letter, underscores this point. The concern of his message was above all to teach others how they might 'know God and him whom he sent, Jesus Christ' (John 17:3). In this spirit John concludes his letter:

> We also know that the Son of God has come and has given us discernment to know the One who is true. We are in the One who is true, for we are in Jesus Christ, his Son. He is the true God and eternal life. Children, be on your guard against idols.   (1 John 5:20–1)

The unfaithful people

In the first letter to the Thessalonians Paul congratulated his believers because they had been given the grace to turn from idols to the true God (1 Thess. 1:9–10). In this passage he is dealing with the first stage of conversion, which begins with baptism. But John was writing to believers who had received baptism long before, admonishing them to continue to be on their guard against idols. This was something they were able to do, he says, only because they had come to know the true God in Jesus Christ. To be on one's guard against idols, discerning and acknowledging the true God afresh each day, is an ongoing part of a believer's life. We are always caught up in this turn-about and must over and over again let go of our idols and turn to the one true God.

Gradually, by a slow process, it became clear to Israel that there is only one God. In the most ancient texts of the Bible every nation seems as a matter of course to have a god of its own. Israel was entitled to its God, just as the other nations had their gods. In time it became clear that those other gods were mere idols, without significance, and that the God of Israel was the one universal God, a God for everyone, the true and ever-faithful God, apart from whom there is no God: 'Hear, O Israel! Yahweh is our God, the one God, Yahweh alone. Therefore, love your God with all your heart, with all your soul, and with all your strength' (Deut. 6:4–5). He towers over all these other little gods so much that no image whatever can or may be made of him. He cannot be captured or tied down in space-bound forms. But he, 'I am who am' (Exod. 3:14), exists for Israel by his love and his power. His face cannot be seen by mortal eyes (Exod. 33:29); his name may not be misused (Exod. 20:7), and in time would not be uttered at all. The result is that today we no longer know how to say his name correctly (the usual pronunciation, 'Yahweh', is merely a somewhat shaky conjecture that is not convincing from a scholarly viewpoint). He is the Unexpressed and Inexpressible who will be known by people only as they actually live by the covenant he makes with them. It is a covenant that will remain throughout the centuries, in which the faithfulness and patience of God will always win over the unfaithfulness of human beings.

Still, Israel's continuing temptation was always to slide away again from their distant and invisible God to the much more material forms of religious worship followed by neighbouring nations. For centuries the unending conversion of Israel was to occur on this level, because this was always its greatest temptation. The continuing question was, would Israel for a time remain faithful to the pledge once given to Yahweh, or would it, in the raw language of the prophets, again go 'whoring' after idols? Over and over Israel would need prophets to point out its pathology and to call attention to the fact that, often unknowingly, it was again yielding to the temptation. For going back and forth between Yahweh and the idols was much easier than remaining steadfastly loyal to the seemingly unreal God of Israel, whose greatest acts of redemption ever threatened to sink into oblivion. The rites of nature religion were also much more attractive than a naked faith in the Unapproachable.

So idolatry always remained as a quiet, hidden undercurrent in the life of the believing nation. Over and over Israel needed to be liberated from this idolatry, because they were always in grave danger of slipping and sinking back into it and sometimes of being totally under its control. From time to time a prophet forcefully intervened. Elijah, for example, challenged Yahweh and Baal to a contest on Mount Carmel, and it was time again for God to say clearly, in view of all the people, whether or not he was the true and living God or merely a slumbering, absent and even perhaps a dead idol himself.

But generally, and long before things became too bad, God intervenes personally. He himself sets the scene for this intervention and comes in person to act in our life. One way or another it always reproduces the philosophy or the dynamism of every conversion. For example, the prophet Hosea described it strikingly:

Says Yahweh: 'Therefore I will hedge in her way with thorns and erect a wall against her so that she cannot find it anymore. If she still runs after her lovers she shall not overtake them; if she looks for them she shall not find them.' Then she shall say, 'I will go back to my first husband, for it was better with me then than now.' (Hos. 2:5–6)

'I will go back' – it is the standard Old Testament expression for conversion, translated in the Greek of the Septuagint by *metanoein*. The symbolic story of the unfaithful bride who retraces her steps to return to her first husband expresses graphically what the Bible means by conversion:

On that day it will be, says Yahweh, that she will call me 'my husband' and never again 'my Baal'. I will remove from her mouth the names of the Baals, so that they will never be mentioned again . . . I will espouse you to me forever, in right and in justice, in goodness and love; I will espouse you in inviolable faithfulness, and you will learn to know Yahweh.   (Hos. 2:16–19)

Jesus, as the successor and greatest of the prophets of the Old Testament, had to appear anew to wean his people away from the temptation presented by a religion caught fast in ritualism. Accordingly, the difficulty Jesus faced was a double one. In the first place, he came to bring the definitive message of good news, something not every Jew was prepared to listen to. But also his preaching took place at a time in history when some of the people had less expectation of such divine intervention than ever before. It was Jesus' calling to disclose the true God at his most mysterious: the love between Father, Son and Holy Spirit. He was also to proclaim the definitive and ultimate redemption of the people of God and to seal it with his own life and death. However, this happened at a time when the ruling class of the Jewish people was cut off from God by its self-assurance and its loss of vision of fulfilment of the promised salvation. They boasted of their historic credentials: 'We are children of Abraham' (John 8:39), or of their exceptional knowledge of the Torah: 'This crowd knows nothing about the Torah' (John 7:49), an attitude which earned them a cutting answer from Jesus, 'God can raise up children for Abraham from these stones' (Luke 3:8). That is to say, it is the love of God itself that is important, not the claims and titles to the love of God they presume to have. Only grace is important. Actually the message of Jesus was extremely simple. It merely extended the line drawn by the prophets before him. But that message was to be his downfall. For the Yahweh whom the Jews of his day honoured with almost fanatic veneration had been remodelled by them into a false god with such care that they were no longer able to recognize him in the person of Jesus and his Father.

The infant church of Jesus was also forced to deal with this temptation. Christianity had barely taken root, and the good news had only just begun to bear fruit, when the same temptation emerged, with the accompanying possibility of slipping away into various forms of idolatry. Paul especially had to contend with this. To counter a legalistic interpretation of the

Torah he repeatedly tried to make plain to his believers why the letter of the Law is unable to redeem anyone, and how only faith and self-surrender are able to bring this about. In doing this he expresses his deepest conviction and probably his personal experience as well, namely 'that grace may be grace' (Rom. 4:16; 11:6). Also, among the newly baptized, the people who had recently broken with paganism, the danger arose that they would go back to the religious forms they had only recently left. They had turned to Jesus, but their old religion had not disappeared. It remained in their religious subconscious as a seductive mirage. This obviously irritated Paul; his pen shook for a moment when he tried to explain to them how in that way they were actually betraying the true God whom they had only recently come to know:

> Certainly, at a time when you did not know God you became slaves to things that by nature are not gods; but now that you have come to know God, or rather to be known by God, how can you turn back again to the weak and elementary teachings, whose slaves you would again become? You are observing days, months, seasons, and years. I am afraid on your account that perhaps I laboured for you in vain (Gal. 4:8–11) ... You were running so well; who came to obstruct you and stop you from following the truth? (Gal. 5:7).

Idols for today

Paul is certainly not joking; he is really serious. However, the question we have to raise is whether such an admonition is still applicable to us today. Perhaps we think that, at least in our countries, twenty centuries of Christianity have averted the danger of idolatry for good. But there are many kinds of idols, and the most dangerous ones are not those we fashion with our hands, but those we unconsciously carry with us in our heads. Do we perhaps have today a piety that has little or nothing to do with the working of the Spirit in us? – a religiosity that is possibly innate in us but which, for this reason, makes it hard for us to recognize the true God in Jesus? We too may slip, sometimes very subtly, toward practices, notions, inner states that have nothing to do with the good news of Jesus and, accordingly, afford little room for grace. On the contrary, these may paralyse the grace of God in our hearts. This idolatrous bent, which kept emerging among the Jews of the Old Testament, also surfaces in us. It is like a disease, the germ of which we constantly carry with us and which may so do its insidious work in us that suddenly, before we are aware of it, it becomes more powerful in us than the Word of God.

We carry with us many forms of natural religion, legalistic observance and ritualism. Most people have a vague universal sense of God. There is a pantheistic god, and a god of romanticism. There is also a god for pharisees – a god to whom Jesus was relentlessly opposed – who would place all certainty and trust in ourselves. Any such god stands in our way and makes it hard for us to see the real God and to find our rest in him alone. Anything, even the finest things, can be distorted; anything can be put to the service of the little god we carry around with us. Genuine grace can also be subtly bent and offered up again, and simultaneously nullified, in honour of our idol. Even the Word of God can be falsified, as Paul shows (2 Cor. 4:2). After all, it can serve us as a pretext for not committing ourselves to God. We can manipulate God's own Word so cleverly that it becomes a wall that grace can no longer penetrate.

It is always a blessing to become aware of this, if only momentarily, as a possibility or risk that it could happen. For illusions in this area are countless. Virtue, generosity or the yearning for perfection or holiness, liturgy or prayer techniques, also that which we deem to be our most intimate prayer or even the most sacred principles of morality – any of these can imply a flight away from God, a desperate attempt to ignore his voice, to hide ourselves from his presence or from what he has to say to us. Our efforts on behalf of others and for the Church of Jesus can also be no more than a kind of flight far away from our deeper self, and far from God, and from the voice in our heart. Theology, modern or classical, can also be an excuse, an alibi, and permit us to get swamped in a rarefied world of insights and concepts where real life cannot bubble up any more. 'Are you a theologian?' asked a hermit of Mount Athos of a monk from the West who had introduced himself as such. 'Ah, a saint is a real flower. But compared with a saint a theologian is only an artificial flower. It imitates a flower's rich display of colour but spreads no fragrance, and bears no fruit.'

We must honestly admit that we all run this risk, and admit too that for a time we have yielded to this illusion, now and then burning a few grains of incense to our idol. But it is also grace – and for many of us the first grace that comes inescapably our way – when gradually we begin to see that for long periods of our life we have remained captive to this illusion and have somewhere lost contact with grace, hence with God, while we sacrificed generously to our little idol. This is anything but a tragic situation: first, because it is a rather frequent occurrence, so frequent in fact that we would almost venture to say that for the majority it is a normal stage; secondly, because God himself allows it to happen this way. For the time being he settles for it, and this 'for the time being' can last a long time. Anyway, we would not call our 'false god' by the name of God if it did not have something to do with the true God, if it were not a sign or an indication of him, a footprint of God here below that could admittedly put us on a false track but possibly also on the right track. After all, for long centuries God has tirelessly been at work setting these numerous footprints of himself in his creation. He did it among countless pagans in the past; he does it also among the pagans of today, even in the pagan that lurks in every one of us under the guise of faith.

To curse God

In such situations God distinguishes himself by his disarming patience. He sometimes allows the process to go on for years, and then all at once he enters our life unexpectedly, or storms in like a tornado to dethrone all these idols and to shatter them at one stroke. This is the finest, also the worst, thing that can happen to us. Initially it is bad. It is a very painful, even a shattering, temptation. The more our idol unconsciously meant to us, the more rapidly and clearly it now strikes us as the worst blasphemy that ever arose in our heart:

God does not exist, God is dead. And it is true: the God to whom I burned incense for years does not in fact exist. He never really existed, except in my imagination. That God is dead. And, insofar as he is not yet dead, he will at some time have to be executed so that I may achieve contact with, and attention for, the one true God. I had fashioned and set up that idol myself. It was merely 'the work of my hands', as the Bible calls the idols (e.g. Isa. 40:19–20), a bit of gold-plating, a piece of stone, a fragment of ritualism. It was all very well-intentioned but it is totally inadequate when I come to tune in to the wavelength of grace or to become even slightly aware of the real and living God.

A believing, involved life that is in many ways devoted to the kingdom of Jesus can also unconsciously carry with it many forms of idolatry. Without our knowing it, this too may be merely the work of our hands. We measure it by an ideal we have made for ourselves, one we impose on ourselves and others, one for which we are prepared to do a lot and which we attempt to realize with mounting intensity. A careful study of bidding prayers used in public worship today would furnish us with innumerable examples of this very subtle form of idolatry, self-worship not excluded. From time to time we sense that this ideal is a size too big for us and continues to elude us. Thank God, it must and will elude us. We cannot bend the real God to our own will. He is simply not within our reach. The fact that virtue somewhere eludes us, and God with it, is the hopeful sign that in fact something other than the idol we are pursuing is in play. The pain of this loss and of our repeated failure is the tiny, almost invisible, crack through which grace may trickle into our lives. It is a great pity if we then try to seal the crack to prove for the umpteenth time to ourselves, and to God, that if only we now begin to do our very best there is a chance we shall succeed – until our boat again springs a leak and the new crack gives God and his grace another chance.

Transferring from an idol to the true God always brings with it a moment of panic in which we are exposed to the extremely painful temptation of thinking that perhaps God is dead. Or, if he should in fact be alive, that he is no God but a terrifying and useless absurdity. At this point we end up

with blasphemy and a curse. This happens in the heart of
Scripture, but in some books of the Bible blasphemy does not
in fact fall from the blue. For just as the Bible knows of
idolatry, so it knows the temptation of rebellion against the
true God, of cursing and blasphemy. The most startling example of this is the book of Job. It trembles and teems with
curses, curses which we may assume are not completely
foreign to God. After all, they occur in Scripture and therefore
have something, somehow, to do with the Holy Spirit who
inspired Scripture. Perhaps a curse is an initial, though still
very flawed and wrong-headed, way of saying something
about God that approaches the truth.

Job was unable to recognize God in the trial which beset
him. Between Job and God there was a wall, the wall of the
established theology of his day. Job had the idea that, because
he was a righteous man, he had the right to be spared all
afflictions and trials. That, after all, was the God-image of his
day: God punishes only sinners, whereas the righteous are
rewarded with prosperity. This is a very limited view of God
indeed, one that has more to do with an idol-image than with
the God who was to deliver up his own Son to affliction on
our behalf. Job lost his bearings totally because, though he
was a good man, he was nevertheless put to the test. He
protested to God, trying to prove his innocence. Neither his
wife nor his friends could offer him any help; they too were
stuck in the theological doctrines of their day. Over and over
again they tried to make clear to him that God was righteous
and judged by the very conventional standards of righteousness of that time. God is punishing you, they say to Job. He
is working with you; and if he feels the need to change some
things in your life, then that is surely proof that you need it.
God wants to turn you around, to make you a better man.
Confess honestly that you have been a sinner and you will
get all your riches back. The God they were talking about is
a highly acceptable God. He is the God of the human system,
built by human standards, to comfort and to pacify, equally
quick to outwit and to deceive. He is a God we can get on
our side and control. He is also the God by means of whom
Job expects to be able to put his friends in their place – in
the same way as his theologian friends are now doing to him

– in order to award himself the first prize. This is the God
we need in order to be admirable, the God on whose applause
we can always count – on condition, of course, that we will
at last *really* do our very best . . .

Job's blasphemies are very closely akin to a certain God-
is-dead-atmosphere we frequently encountered, some thirty
years ago, in modern literature. Jean-Paul Sartre, like Job,
was the eternal anti-God rebel. From time to time this stance
gave him a very caustic but not incorrect view of certain
deformities in the Christian image of God. It is always easier,
after all, to track down an idol than to find the real God.
So, in his autobiography *Les Mots*, he described the religious
posture of his grandfather in these icy terms: 'My grandfather
was too much of an actor not to need a Great Spectator whom
he called God.' Job's idol was also of this sort. Job needed a
God who would approve of him and congratulate him, who
would applaud him for all the good he was doing. And when
God failed to act in this way Job indicted him, challenging
him to a public trial:

> Have I been a fellow-traveller with falsehood, or hastened
> my steps towards deceit? Let him weigh me on accurate
> scales: then he, God, will [have to] recognize my
> integrity . . . Look here is my signature; let the Almighty
> answer me. Let my adversary draft his writ against me.
> Truly, I will carry it on my shoulder . . . I will give him
> an account of my every step and go out to meet him as
> a prince. (Job 31:5–6, 35–7; cf. NJB)

God's answer to Job is full of caustic irony:

> Brace yourself like a fighter,
>   I am going to ask the questions, and you are to inform
> me!
> Do you really want to reverse my judgement,
>   put me in the wrong and yourself in the right?
> Has your arm the strength of God's,
>   can your voice thunder as loud?
> Come on, display your majesty and grandeur,
>   robe yourself in splendour and glory . . .

And I shall be the first to pay you homage,
   since your own right hand is strong enough to save
   you. (Job 40:7–10, 14 NJB)

Those words are really on target, because Job wanted in
fact to be his own saviour. If his own right hand could save
him, Job would not need the true God, would he? Unconsciously Job wanted to be his own saviour, and therefore
his own God, with no more than a little idol to serve him.
Presumably God should have been glad to be a candidate for
that position. However, when the true and living God revealed
himself, he first ran straight into this unconscious attitude of
Job and into an idol he could only dash in pieces. That was
why God acted with such urgency. Job himself says that God's
action was bewildering, that he was attacking him. He states
his complaint loudly:

I was living at peace until he made me totter,
   taking me by the neck to shatter me.
He has set me up as his target:
   he shoots his arrows at me from all sides,
pitilessly pierces my loins,
   and pours my gall out on the ground.
Breach after breach he drives through me,
   charging on me like a warrior . . .
God has wronged me
   and attacked me . . .
He has blocked my path
   and covered my way with darkness . . .
He assails me from all directions . . .
   uproots my hope as he might a tree . . .
His troops have come in force.
God is tearing up the ground from under my feet.
   (Job 16:12–14 NJB; 19:6–8, 10–12)

Did God have any alternative?
How did Job react, and how do we react, to this challenge
from God? It is so hard for us to give up our own trusted idol
in order to convert to the living God that we have only two
choices: either to deny God or to deny ourselves. The choice

is either blasphemy or self-destruction, either 'God is dead' or 'I wish I had never been born'. When our idol lies broken in fragments our confusion is so great, and our vulnerability vis-à-vis the true God so intense, that it is much easier for us to deny him or ourselves – if then God exists, we wish we didn't! – than to risk a genuine encounter with him. Job opened his mouth to curse the day of his birth.

> This is what he said:
> Perish the day on which I was born,
> and the night that told of a boy conceived.
> May that day be darkness,
> may God on high have no thought for it,
> may no light shine on it.   (Job 3:1–4 NJB).

Job, by his own admission, sought to die; as others dig in search of a spring of living water, so he dug around seeking death. He pleaded that God might annihilate, might destroy him:

> May it please God to crush me,
> to give his hand free play and do away with me!
> This . . . would give me comfort,
> a thrill of joy in unrelenting pain.   (Job 6:9–10 NJB)

This pain-filled thrill of Job is not hard to understand. If God were to take Job's life away by violence, then God would be the guilty party and furnish proof of his own wrong. Job would have avenged himself against God, remaining the bigger and the better of the two, by means of his own innocent death, a death for which God alone would be responsible.

Earlier we alluded to modern literature. Well, Job's curses again remind us of Jean-Paul Sartre, though the latter was not a believer. He was an unbeliever and wanted to prove the correctness of his unbelief. But in the attempt he inadvertently fell into the same dilemma in which Job was caught. The God whom Sartre rejected was also an idol, a god who would have to applaud when someone behaved well and punish when he did wrong. Such a god would prove he did not exist if Sartre could prove that it makes no sense to be good, or to be bad, because good and bad, by the human standards which Sartre naturally applies, are contradictory concepts.

We find a well known attempt at this argument in his play *Le diable et le bon Dieu (The Devil and the Good Lord)*. In this play he introduced a medieval army commander named Goetz, an unbeliever who, to give force to his unbelief, decided one day to do only evil from then on. To his astonishment he could not succeed. No matter how hard he worked at doing evil, the effect each time was good. This led him to conclude that he must go still further down the road of evil and rebellion against God. So he decided that from then on he would do only good and become a saint. But this, too, had the opposite effect; all the good he did had evil consequences. Goetz believed he had thus furnished proof that neither good nor evil exists and that therefore God does not exist. So, in the end he cried out to a priest:

> Heaven does not even know my name. I used to ask every minute what I could be in the eyes of God. Now I know the answer – nothing. God doesn't see me. God doesn't hear me. God doesn't know me. You see this emptiness above our heads? It's God. You see this crack in the door? It's God. You see this hole in the ground? It's God again. Silence – it's God; absence – it's God. God is the isolation of human beings. There's nothing but me. I alone decided what's evil. I alone invented the good. It's I alone who deceived, who did miracles. It's I who am accusing myself today and who alone can absolve myself, me, a human being. If God exists, man is nothing. If man exists . . .

Here Sartre stops. The words 'Dieu est néant' ('God is nothing') did not flow from his pen. And rightly so. If we read this page as we read Job's curses in the Bible, we can find in it one of the most moving confessions of God the literature of this century has produced. Behind this out-spokenly negative theology there certainly lurks a very distinct experience of God.

Sartre acknowledges, in his autobiography, that just once he did meet God, but he believed this brief encounter was enough for him to repudiate God for ever. It occurred during an incident that took place when he was still little. Sartre was playing with matches in the bathroom of his grandparents' home. In his awkwardness he burned a small rug, and for a moment thought the whole room would go up in flames. 'I was in the process of covering up my crime when suddenly God saw me. I felt his gaze inside my head and on my hands. I whirled about, horribly visible, a live target.' Sartre thinks that in that moment he said 'No' to God, 'and he never looked at me again'.*

From then on even God's glance became unbearable, as it was for Job who, long before Sartre, accused God of the same thing.

> What are human beings that you should take them so
>   seriously,
>   subjecting them to your scrutiny,
> that morning after morning you should examine them
>   and at every instant test them?
> Will you never take your eyes off me
>   long enough for me to swallow my spittle?
> Suppose I have sinned, what have I done to you,
>   you tireless watcher of humanity?
> Why do you choose me as your target?
>   Why should I be a burden to you?
> Can you not tolerate my sin,
>   not overlook my fault?
> For soon I shall be lying in the dust,
>   you will look for me and I shall be no more.
>   (Job 7:17–21 NJB)

Just as Sartre saw himself as God's live target, so also Job complains that he has become the bull's eye for God's horrifying action. In his eyes God is a monster, an inhuman 'watcher of mankind'. This last expression is perhaps the most painful curse Job could conceive. Turning God's own words around, he shoots them back at God. For in the Bible God is often called the *Nôser Israel*, the Watcher of Israel, who lovingly

---

*J. P. Sartre, *The Words* (New York 1964), p. 102

watches his people with a caring fatherly eye. For the moment, however, Job cannot bear that loving look. In a way he cannot understand, that look is killing him.

A hearsay God

But it is also this same look that will be able to restore and eventually heal Job. After endless blasphemies the conclusion of the book of Job finally ends satisfactorily. Through horror and despair Job learned something. It was given him to glimpse the true face of the true God:

> This was the answer Job gave to Yahweh:
> . . . I have spoken without insight
> about things too wonderful for me . . .
> Listen, please, and let me speak,
>   and teach me when I ask you questions.
> I knew you only by hearsay,
>   but now I have seen you with my own eyes
> (Job 42:1–6).

The book of Job does not enlarge on the way Job arrived at this insight, but these few words are enough to give us an inkling. Formerly Job did not know the true God, but actually awaited the action of a little idol he had fashioned himself, in accordance with his own standards and needs, the work of his own hands. The God he knew was either stern or permissive. But then suddenly, in the middle of affliction for which his idol had no solution, he met up with the real God, a consuming fire. It took weeks, and interminable discussions with his friends, before he was able to recognize this God and to read love in his eyes. That look was so different from the look he expected, neither approving or disapproving. It left Job free. That look could only be read as the look of love that never stops. God was always with Job, in prosperity and in distress and misfortune, in sickness and in death. God is not a man-sized being; he did not correspond to Job's desires or fears. God listened to Job attentively and took him as he was, listening not only to his good intentions, but also to his curses, his blasphemies, his desperation. He listened with attentiveness and love. God knew how to handle this despair much better than Job's earlier self-assurance. Now at last Job's eyes could see. Only despair and desperation were able to teach Job something about the true God.

We too know God only from hearsay, sometimes for many years. In affliction we too will first react the way Job did. The true God comes to break down something in us and we resist. God's purpose is to crush our idols. There is in us a self-assurance to which we cling to the point of despair but with which God cannot do anything. He wants to take that assurance away from us. This causes us so much pain, and our disappointment with God is so intense that we are strongly inclined to curse him, that we even begin to doubt his existence, or that in some way we want to get even with him. None of this is too serious. For even in the most embittered curse we still voice something of our faith, and in every blasphemy the true image of God is still somehow present, if only in a hidden and perverse fashion. It is God himself who takes us into his hands, God who – we think – attacks us because he wants to remove that which is dearest to us and to which we are unknowingly attached, heart and soul – the little idol which we have carried with us for years and which we adore as the true God.

We cannot escape this; we are bound, like Sartre or like Job, to become the live target of the living God who breaks us down in order to build us up again. For 'it is he who wounds and it is he who heals' (Job 5:18). In quiet confidence and humble self-surrender we try to accept this reality. And as we wait for it with an almost indiscernible but nevertheless a deep joy, God gradually opens our eyes. His look makes us free to look back. Till now we had known him only from hearsay; soon, very soon, we will have seen him with our eyes.

3

THE POWER OF FAITH

BY FAR THE majority of readers of this book will be 'believers,' that is, people who adhere to the Christian faith. Now 'faith' and 'believer' are two terms which seem fairly clear to us and which we do not easily question. That is so, of course, with numerous words we use regularly, but it has the danger that some of their basic nuances will in time become threadbare, or that secondary meanings begin to play too great a role. Accordingly, it is sometimes helpful to look critically at our everyday use of words.

How shall we speak of faith?

The word 'faith' entails a difficulty arising from the two related adjectives 'believing' and 'non-believing.' As a rule we use these words to denote two sociologically well-defined groups in society. Everywhere one finds believers and non-believers. Accordingly, most people can usually state without hesitation to which of the two groups they belong. It is almost like one's occupation, or nationality, or civil status – something one could put on his or her tax returns, as in fact happens in some countries.

In English we have two other adjectives related to faith or belief which may actually put us on the wrong track: 'credible' and 'credulous'. We call something credible when it seems reasonable and therefore probable. The word unintentionally suggests that faith might have something to do with objective probability. 'Incredible' would then mean improbable. The same ambiguity is present in the use of 'credulous' and 'incredulous'. An incredulous person is someone indisposed to accept what is related as true, someone who takes the standards of probability too seriously, a person to whom one cannot possibly tell tales. A credulous person, on the other hand, does not take the standards of probability seriously enough and therefore seems naive. Here the same root relating to *credo* (I believe) is used in a context of which we may well ask what it has to do with the faith of which the gospel speaks.

When we speak of faith, we think also of Christian doctrines, a way of speaking that tends to take the concept of faith in the direction of an intellectual system. The word 'doctrine' brings to mind a handbook of theology or catechetical instruction in which the Word of God is laid down didactically. A doctrinal expression of the faith is of course of great importance and should be very carefully constructed. But it is just as essential to emphasize the fact that faith differs radically from studying, however exemplarily, a handbook of theological truths. A person may know a great deal about the faith and share a lot of information about it with others without ever having made the decisive step of *surrendering his or her life to Jesus*.

Part of the difficulty comes perhaps from the fact that, in accordance with current church practice, most of us received baptism at a very early age, and so imbibed the faith from childhood. We confess that at our baptism the gift of faith was infused in us. We therefore assume that ever since we have unquestionably been believers. That is in fact the case, but only to a degree. Without wanting to criticize current church practice, we must nevertheless point out that infused faith is no more than a beginning. It must not serve us as an alibi for not concerning ourselves about a personal encounter with Jesus. We could legitimately be baptized at an early age by virtue of the faith of the Church, which was concretely represented at our baptism by our parents and godparents. They took upon themselves the task of assisting the infused, still unconscious, faith of their child or godchild and of guiding its growth toward and into the real faith encounter with Jesus. Apart from this commitment of parents and godparents the Church would never admit children to the sacrament of baptism, because without catechetical instruction the unconscious faith of the child who was baptized would for ever remain dormant and probably be smothered.

We may ask whether in the lives of most Christians this unconscious faith does not remain dormant for a long time because no one deliberately concerns themselves about it, or else people concern themselves in a way that has so little to do with grace that its fruits are barely noticeable. What happens in many cases is that a system of religious doctrines is superimposed on this unconscious faith, purely at the level of the intellect, and at the level of practical conduct a few principles of Christian behaviour are instilled. But we are seldom taught how to 'connect' with the faith conveyed to us earlier, how to 'listen' to the life of grace in us, and how to learn to live and to love on the basis of this life of grace. Then, when the time comes for us, on our part, to pass the faith on to the younger generation we too fall short and in the same way. People who have never discerned the grace of God in their own life, because they have never been taught what to look for, will not be able as parents to convey it to their own children. They will try to pass on a number of religious doctrines together with a conscientious and irreproachable lifestyle, but it is one in which the grace of God barely comes into its own.

The astonishment of Jesus

Faith is not an easy road to travel; nor is it a speedway. It takes time and patience. 'Lord, I do believe; help my unbelief!' (Mark 9:24). To gain a better understanding of faith we have to go back to the gospel, more specifically to the passage in which Jesus praises a person's faith in a way he does nowhere else. I refer to the faith of a Roman centurion, which so astonished Jesus that he said he had never before found such great faith, not even in Israel (Matt. 8:10) The synoptic gospels describe only two situations in which Jesus displayed amazement. In the case of the centurion he was amazed at his faith. In the case of his fellow townspeople in Nazareth Jesus was amazed at their unbelief. Mark expressly states: 'He was amazed at their lack of faith' (Mark 6:6 NJB), adding that Jesus was not able to work miracles there.

Let us pause a moment to consider Jesus' unbelieving audience. This unbelief does in fact deserve amazement. Here are fellow townspeople, people of Nazareth, perhaps Jesus' own neighbours, people who had known him for years. Did we perhaps think that they were in an exceptionally favourable position to know Jesus well, to *fathom* him as it were? Perhaps we have even envied them, thinking it would have been much easier for us to believe in him had we too been his contemporaries and fellow townspeople. But what we learn from the gospel suggests precisely the opposite. And Jesus emphasizes this as though this attitude was self-evident: 'A prophet is despised only in his own country' (Mark 6:4). Humanly speaking, the closer one is to Jesus, the harder it is to believe in him.

The disbelief of the people of Nazareth is surprising for still another reason. It is clear from this passage that those whom Jesus met in the synagogue on the sabbath were among the most devout Jews of that time. Not only do they know the Law, but they are regular worshippers at the synagogue and hence fervent believers. They believe in the Word of God, but still they cannot believe in Jesus. On the contrary, they are offended by his words. And this response shows that they are, if we may put it that way, genuinely the religious sort. Those whose religion did not mean much to them would not have been offended by Jesus' words. They would have smiled perhaps, or shrugged their shoulders, but certainly not been offended, still less would they have wanted to intervene. So, they are clearly devoutly religious folk. But Jesus does not ring any bells in them, his words do not seem credible to them, his miracles do not inspire trust in them. Something in them is shut down and they are unable to unbolt the door. It even seems that the closer they get to Jesus and the more conscientiously they confess their religion and fulfil its requirements, the harder it is for them to surrender to the words and person of Jesus in terms of the faith he wants from them. Indeed, throughout the entire gospel it seems that the less respectable people – publicans, prostitutes and foreigners – have a great advantage in this respect when compared to faithful, believing Jews.

The centurion at whose faith Jesus expresses so much astonishment is precisely of this kind. Not only is he unknown, he is also a foreigner. Not just any impartial foreigner, but an officer of the Roman army of occupation, hence an enemy. He does strike the Jews as an acceptable person, and under that Roman uniform he must have had a heart of gold – one of the gospel writers even tells us that he had built a synagogue in Capernaum (Luke 7:5) – but he is no believing Jew. Yet it is he of all people who was able to give his heart and trust to Jesus – he had in fact received that rare kind of faith that Jesus was looking for with such eagerness. A few moments' study of that passage can tell us more about that centurion's faith.

The first thing that strikes us about him is his humility, his sense of his own smallness. He found himself in a situation of neediness and distress; he cried to Jesus for help. A slave who was very dear to him was fatally ill. But he could have taken a different course. As an officer in an army of occupation he could have summoned that famed miracle man to come to him. Instead, he took it upon himself to travel a day's journey to meet Jesus. Moreover, he did not feel he had any claims on Jesus, not even the right to have him come to his house as a visitor. He was just an outsider. When Jesus calmly announced that he would come to his house to heal his servant, his immediate reaction was, 'Lord, I am not worthy'. He was uncircumcised, an unbeliever, and though he had had a synagogue built he was not a member of the chosen people. He assumed a position of minimal importance and confessed that 'littleness' before Jesus: 'Lord, I am not worthy that you should come under my roof'. *Only speak the word and shall be healed*

The second striking element in his attitude is his unbounded confidence in Jesus. So many Jews had doubts about Jesus. But this man was completely certain that Jesus could and would heal his slave. Such a conviction made sense only if the centurion somehow sensed that a personal link already existed between Jesus and himself. The centurion had a premonition that Jesus would help him. This is already a great deal more than mere belief in Jesus' healing power or in Jesus' message. For the centurion to believe that Jesus would do it because Jesus wanted to help him shows that something had grown in the centurion's heart in relation to Jesus – something comparable perhaps to friendship. Such trust had, in turn, a profound impact on Jesus. It became all the harder for him to refuse his intervention. The centurion's cry for help was brought home to him in a very personal way.

Finally there was in the centurion a sense of the power of Jesus' word: 'Only say the word and my servant will be healed' (Matt. 8:8). It was superfluous, the centurion believed, for Jesus to appear in person; it was enough for him to utter a command. This reaction is characteristic of an officer who knows from experience what it means to issue and follow orders. One word is enough: 'Come,' and he comes; 'Go,' and he goes. So the centurion, with his characteristic Roman military sensitivity and despite the differences, came close here to the kind of believing surrender and obedience every Jew sought to practise in relation to the Word of God and the power present in it. For him faith was complete self-surrender to the word of one he trusted, his 'yes' to the Word of God.

Endorsement and self-surrender

The Hebrew word for faith (*emûnah*) derives from the stem *emeth*, faithfulness, one of God's greatest attributes. God is merciful and faithful (*hesed we' emeth*, Gen. 24:27). We might as well say, tender and tough. For *emeth* evokes the image of a rock on which we can lean or build. God will not move; we can always count on him. Our faith is the act of leaning on the toughness or 'sturdiness' of God. The liturgical word 'Amen' has the same stem. To say 'Amen' is above all to believe; it is the act of affirming the sturdiness of God as it comes through to us from his Word or from the person of Jesus. The Apocalypse of John says of Jesus that he is at once *amen* and *pistos* – faithful (Rev. 3:14). He is faithful in two directions. It is his privilege boundlessly and, as it were, recklessly to lean against his Father, because he as no other may count on his Father's power and 'sturdiness'. Similarly in his relation to us he becomes the eminently sturdy and powerful one against whom we on our part may lean just as recklessly and boundlessly.

The centurion's faith welled up from the distress he suffered. It was, however, especially trust in Jesus and surrender to his Word, to the point of obeying it. Accordingly, faith is

not merely or primarily a matter of saying 'Amen' to religious
doctrines about Jesus but of saying 'Amen' to Jesus himself,
together with all the power given him by the Father, an act
which implies our total commitment to him. It is therefore
important, not only that we believe there is a God, or that
we believe him when he tells us something, but that we believe
in God ('in' with the Greek or Latin accusative of movement,
as it is prepared in the Apostle's Creed – Greek: *pisteuein eis
ton Theon*; Latin: *credere in Deum*). It is a faith in going toward
God, a faith that pulls my whole self along with it. This faith
has two sides, it is an *exit* from my self and an *entry* into God.
It is like the faith of the centurion, with whose words, every
day, I can hang my whole life on the saving word of Jesus:
'Just say the word, Lord, and I will be healed.'

   Such a faith implies a radical turn-about. By this faith a
person is lured out of himself or herself; one learns to forget
and to surrender oneself in order to get within reach of God's
living and omnipotent Word, with all its implications. One of
the implications is that in faith we receive power from God
himself. For faith is not only the way in which we may cleave
to God and eventually be with him; it is also the way God
opens up in us for the release of his own power and omnipotence in order to do his mighty works everywhere in the
world.

A miracle-working faith

Earlier we read in the gospel that Jesus could not do miracles
in his home town because of the unbelief of its inhabitants.
It was not that Jesus had lost his almighty power but that it
was curbed by unbelief. It is also impossible for Jesus to act
in our life as long as we cannot, from within our weakness to
be sure but in full confidence, fully surrender to him. Jesus
confronts every human being in the fullness of his love and
almighty power, but most people are not attuned to him, and
so he cannot act. The object of Jesus' search is our deepest
distress and blind self-surrender; that is the terrain on which
today also, by way of our faith and his almighty power, he
seeks to accomplish miracles. In the gospel Jesus was happily
surprised each time he encountered this faith, no matter in

whose life he discovered it. 'Go back then,' he told the centurion, 'let this be done for you, as your faith demands' (Matt. 8:13 NJB).

This is not the only time Jesus attributed his own action as a worker of miracles to the faith of the people who heard him. Miracles turn out to be not just his work – they lie somehow within the reach of those who ask for them. Often Jesus himself admitted that the healing he was in process of bringing about had to be attributed to the faith of the person being healed: 'Your faith has saved you' (Matt. 9:22; Luke 8:48; 17:19; 18:42 and *passim*). Before the great faith displayed by the Canaanite woman Jesus even gave up his own will in order to fulfil the woman's desire: 'Woman, you have great faith! Let your desire be granted' (Matt. 15:28). Thus Jesus himself concedes that he will yield to the faith of one who asks him for something. Just as unbelief paralyses Jesus, so faith liberates him.

This implies a strange dialogue of faith between God and man. God as the primary actor speaks first and then expects of us that, the moment we have come under the spell of his Word, we shall surrender to it. But this has barely taken place before God, as it were, makes himself the humble servant of the believer who has made a complete surrender to him. Not only does God remain omnipotent, but the person who believes participates in that omnipotence. True, Mary first surrendered to the Word of God spoken to her by the angel Gabriel: 'Let it happen to me as you said' (Luke 1:38). But in the second stage of the dialogue of faith God turns this sentence around and plays it back to us: 'According to your faith let it be done to you' (Matt. 9:29), 'Let your desire be granted' (Matt. 15:28). Thus our faith is like the womb that is made fertile by the almighty Word of God, and in turn participates in God's omnipotence the moment this Word has been received in personal surrender. Nothing is then excluded in advance: 'Everything is possible for one who has faith' (Mark 9:24).

Faith is always amply sufficient. It is true the centurion said to Jesus: 'Just say one word and my servant will be healed' (Luke 7:7), but in another context the request came from Jesus: Just believe a little. 'If you have faith the size of a mustard seed' (Matt. 17:20), a miracle will happen. It is clear that at this point the object of our faith is not primarily a set of doctrines we are able to articulate and to confess. This only happens at the second stage, a stage down the line and one that flows from the actual experience of faith. The object of faith here is primarily the miraculous power of God as it is available to each of us and to the entire world in the Word of God, in the Church's redemptive signs, and above all in the Risen Lord, Jesus Christ. After all we believe in the power forever released in Jesus' resurrection, a power designed to be transmitted through our faith to every one of us and to the whole world.

Thus through our faith the power of Jesus' resurrection from the dead is made available to all. This is the language of Paul who, on behalf of the believers in Ephesus, begged for this insight:

> May the God of our Lord Jesus Christ, the Father of glory, give you a spirit of wisdom and perception of what is revealed, to bring you to full knowledge of him. May he enlighten the eyes of your mind so that you can see . . . how extraordinarily great is the power that he has exercised for us believers; this accords with the strength of his power at work in Christ, the power which he exercised in raising him from the dead and enthroning him at his right hand in heaven. (Eph. 1:17–20 NJB)

Faith renders us open to the power of God. Accordingly, it is the liberation of our most intimate self, the redemption of our heart. It is as if God pulls aside a bolt in our deepest self and a door opens. Through this opening he can flow into the deepest dimensions of our self and pull it along in the loving grip and restorative power of his omnipotence. This resembles the much grander and more spectacular manner in which, on Easter morning, Jesus was raised from the dead by the overwhelming power of the glory of the Father. On a different scale but along the same lines, the coming of faith is such an event, one that seizes not only our minds but our entire human existence. From this experience we emerge very small and lost, small to ourselves, before others and before God, but not at all crushed. On the contrary, we are lifted up by this boundless confidence in him who 'by the power at work within us is able to accomplish abundantly far more than all we can ask or imagine' (Eph. 3:20 NRSV), and ready therefore for the miracles the Lord Jesus would again seek to accomplish through our faith even today. Beyond doubt, God is unceasingly at work in the Church and in the world. Only our faith can discern these continuing miracles and ultimately play its own role in them. Could we effectively participate in God's work in any other way? And as believers are we not called to open a door to miracles in the Church of today? Every believer must allow this miraculous power and faithfulness of God to become a reality in his or her life. For that matter, one's own faith is the very first miracle of God – just as the centurion himself was a miracle of God long before his servant was healed. Our faith (Greek: *pistis*) after all points to the God whom the Bible defines as *the* faithful one: *pistos* (Rev. 1:5), the One who remains unwaveringly and immovably sturdy and faithful in relation to us, the rock we can lean against, the foundation on which we can build.

Each time God lets us know personally that miracles are taking place in and around us, this is a sign we are in the process of release from unbelief and are beginning to believe. For God works miracles not only so that people should believe, but above all because of the people who believe and are confidently open to his power. Miracles arise from their faith and slip from their hands before they realize it. Faith, after all, is this seeking, groping experience of God's omnipotent love; it is the grateful realization that one may oneself become a miraculous offshoot of his omnipotence and, to the degree he wants this, a luminous sign to all people.

4

GROWING BY BEING TESTED

THE FACT THAT God is unwaveringly faithful to us, as we saw in the previous chapter, will be evident especially in times of testing. There is no faith that is not tested, just as there is no tree that does not need to be pruned in order to produce more fruit (John 15:2). Does not Scripture say continually that God's faithfulness is made real especially in times of testing? And also that it is most necessary for us to be tested in order to grow in faith? Let us first listen to Paul:

> No testing has overtaken you that is not common to everyone. God is faithful and he will not let you be tested beyond your strength, but with the testing he will also provide the way out so that you may be able to endure it. (1 Cor. 10:13 NRSV)

Then listen especially to the famous words with which James, rather abruptly, begins his letter:

> My brothers and sisters, whenever you face trials of any kind, consider it nothing but joy, because you know that the testing of your faith produces endurance; and let endurance have its full effect, so that you may be mature and complete, lacking in nothing. (Jas. 1:2 NRSV)

The weakness of the flesh

But is it possible for humans to be continually tested, to be continually a miracle of God's grace? The gospels show us in many ways that our advances on this road seldom proceed along a straight line. When in the night before his passion

Jesus discreetly alluded to the faltering way in which his disciples would at first attempt to follow him, Peter, as usual, firmly protested: 'Though all become deserters because of you, I will never desert you.' And when Jesus said that he would deny him, Peter did not for a moment hesitate to make an even stronger claim: 'Even though I must die with you, I will not deny you' (Matt. 26:30–5 NRSV). Soon after this he failed, and that despite Jesus' double warning: 'Stay awake and pray that you may not come into the time of trial; the spirit indeed is willing, but the flesh is weak' (Matt. 26:41 NRSV).

These words of Jesus apply to all of us. Even though from time to time our spirit is fervent, our flesh remains incurably weak. No one can escape the split, even the conflict, between the two. It is a part of all Christian experience to have to live between fervency and weakness – that is to say, in temptation. Peter, who was destined to be the main witness of Jesus' resurrection and the pre-eminent leader in the Church, had to be the first to be confronted with temptation, even the first to fall short and to fail in a situation of temptation. His denial in the night of passion hardly came as a surprise. He had failed many times before. For example, when Jesus predicted for the first time his suffering and resurrection, Peter immediately tried to talk Jesus out of such 'evil' thoughts: 'God forbid it, Lord! This must never happen to you!' But Jesus turned and said to Peter: 'Get behind me, Satan! You are a stumbling block to me; for you are setting your mind not on divine things but on human things' (Matt. 16:21–3). Only when the heavenly Father assisted Peter in a special way was he able to confess that Jesus was the Christ, the Son of the living God – a truth that totally escaped him when he limited himself to flesh and blood (Matt. 16:17), that is, as long as he leaned on human insight.

Accordingly, for him to be first in the Church and first in love for Jesus, Peter had to be the first to be tempted. Jesus himself expressly made a connection between the two when he predicted Peter's denial: 'Simon, Simon, listen! Satan has demanded to sift all of you like wheat, but I have prayed for you that your own faith may not fail; and you, when once you have turned back, strengthen your brothers' (Luke 22:31–2).

In those few sentences we recognize the themes that are engaging us in the early chapters of this book: temptation – being sifted by a winnowing-fan is a metaphor of the great temptation at the end of time (Matt. 3:12); the faith that is being tested; and the conversion that follows the experience of being tested. Only after Peter had come through this process of temptation and conversion was he qualified by virtue of his own experience to strengthen and comfort his brothers as they went through the same process. Not until he had come through his own time of testing did Peter discover how weakness and grace have to balance each other in every one of Jesus' disciples.

This needs to be emphasized. In his search for a leader Jesus was not looking for a model of virtue or perfection which Christians of all later times could then look at and, according to their ability, imitate. For this purpose Peter would certainly not have been a good choice. The few indications of his character shown in the gospels are clear and colourful enough for us to grasp that he was a thoroughly decent but rather rough fisherman, who showed a tendency to act impetuously and rashly, and did not always manage to control his feelings. He clearly loved Jesus, however, and was passionately attached to him. The more mistakes he made, and the more reprimands he incurred, the more he came to love Jesus. No, Peter was not a model of obvious virtue. But he *was* able to pass on an experience of things that happened to him because of Jesus and to which he could testify for all time. To be sure, temptation made him stumble, but Jesus marvellously rescued him from the depths of his fall.

All this started at the time of his call, the story of which clearly conveys the dialogue between the weakness of Peter and the power of grace (Luke 5:1-11). At the beginning of the story Peter was barely involved. He had had a bad night. It was not that he had a hard time falling asleep. He did not sleep at all; he was out on a boat all night trying to catch fish. But the catch was totally disappointing. He could not have been in the best of humour as he checked his nets not far from where a young rabbi was preaching. If Peter listened at all, it was absentmindedly. At this time he did not yet know Jesus. Nor did Jesus seem to have noticed Peter. Still it was Jesus who made the first move. He stepped into Peter's boat and asked him to put out a little way from the shore. The crowd was pressing in on Jesus and he wanted to finish his preaching in the boat from a distance. It must have struck Peter that the rabbi was making an appeal to him, speaking to him as man to man. He requested a service, something to which Peter could not have been insensitive. He complied, and as a result could no longer avoid paying attention to Jesus' words.

Then followed Jesus' second move. The moment he finished speaking he invited Peter to start fishing: 'Put out into the deep water and let down your nets for a catch.' By this time some measure of understanding had grown up between Jesus and Peter. Peter was sure that there were no fish in that area but found it hard to refuse Jesus' request. He yielded, protesting for the moment and pointing to the lack of success during the night but then agreeing. Did he sense perhaps that Jesus might do something about the disappointing outcome of the night? We do not know, but at this point Peter addressed Jesus in a very personal and almost intimate manner, even though prospects were bleak: 'If you say so, I will let down the nets.' This element of trust in Peter enabled Jesus to make his next move – the miraculous catch of fish. Peter caught more fish than he ever dared to hope for, more even than the nets could hold. He needed help, and two boats were filled to the point where they nearly sank. Peter could now thank Jesus for the unforeseen and unlikely miracle, but in the meantime something much deeper had taken place in him. The miraculous catch of fish did not just help him get over a bad night; far beyond that human disappointment this event touched a much more serious, more fundamental failure in Peter's life. Through the miracle Jesus unexpectedly touched sin in the heart of Peter. 'When Simon Peter saw it, he fell down at Jesus' knees, saying, "Go away from me, Lord, for I am a sinful man!" ' (Luke 5:8).

Peter no longer said '*Rabbi*' (Master), but '*Kyrios*' (Lord). It is the name reserved for God himself. In Jesus Peter recognized the presence and person of God. But at the same moment he realized that he himself was a sinner. This is the ordinary course of events. The moment Jesus reveals himself our sin also immediately comes to light. And conversely, it is not possible for us really to gain insight into our sin until we come to stand in the light of Jesus. Thus Peter was confronted with the failure that *he himself* was and that he had the courage to expose to Jesus. It was the most secret, the most poignant, failure that he carried with him. Suddenly he knew it; he himself was a sad case, a sinner – that was all. And as a sinner, he thought, he could have nothing to do with Jesus and Jesus had nothing in common with him. 'Go away from me, Lord, for I am a sinful man.'

But what happened was the exact reverse: it was precisely this confession by Peter that enabled Jesus to make his last move to check-mate Peter. Unless, of course, it was Jesus who was made check-mate by Peter's confession. For, in the acknowledgement and confession of sin, both parties gave in. The moment Peter confessed his sin Jesus could act and forgive. The moment the wound was laid open, Jesus could exercise his healing power and rebuild Peter, as it were from the bottom up: 'From now on you will be catching people . . .' The fact that at the same moment in which he called Peter, he should come upon his sin is not at all surprising. For Jesus was not looking for extraordinary qualities in his first and closest disciples. He was seeking out their weakness, their unconscious failure, their unsuspected lack, all those sick spots in human beings who needed his love, who could only be relieved and carried by his love, and in whom his love could manifest itself as omnipotence. After all, Jesus came among us to take our weakness upon himself and to transmute it into strength. He died to sin once and for all and was raised from death to new life by his Father.

God's power manifest in weakness

One of the most ancient and succinct credal statements of the Church, cited by Paul in his second letter to the Corinthians, defines very clearly this strange but saving tension between temptation and victory, between weakness and strength, and applies it to Jesus' Easter event: 'For he was crucified in weakness, but lives by the power of God' (2 Cor. 13:4). Jesus was crucified and died on account of human weakness, weakness he had taken upon himself to the ultimate degree; but from that condition of weakness he arose and now lives by the power of God. In this weakness, which is our weakness, he encountered God's power, and from it he was raised to new life. So also for Jesus, human weakness became the way by which he could meet the love and power of his Father.

For that reason it is inescapable for a disciple of Jesus, one who wants to walk the road that Jesus walked, in turn to stand in his own weakness and therefore in temptation. Since Jesus suffered and endured our weakness, and died on account of it in order to rise from it, the power of God lies deeply concealed in every human weakness like a seed that will germinate in faith and surrender. As long as we go on resisting our weakness, the power of God cannot come into its own within us. Of course we can chip away at our weakness, but this does not really help. For the miracle of God's omnipotence and our conversion does not lie within our reach. Sometimes, it is true, we attempt to solve our problems ourselves with the aid of a lot of goodwill and noble intentions. We do our best, in our own strength, to live a virtuous and just life. We live on good intentions and willpower, for a time we try to thrive on our honesty, our generosity – until we threaten to fall apart. Thank God! For if we succeeded we would remain outside the conversion-process and continue to be governed by our illusions and our idols, with barely a notion of authentic faith – be it as minute as a mustard seed. The fact is that we even *have* to suffer shipwreck on the road of good intentions in order that we may experience our weakness, the weakness in which the power of God can unfold its strength. This is what happened in Peter's life; as long as he counted himself among the righteous he could not recognize Jesus, but the moment Jesus began really to reveal himself to him, Peter immediately found himself to be one of the sinners. Jesus in fact did not come for the righteous but only for sinners – as he himself clearly announced (Matt. 9:13). We are dealing here with an essential part of every Christian experience – perhaps the most important condition for being touched by grace or for being able to tune in on the wavelength of grace.

Paul, too, formulates this fact in virtually the same words. When his adversaries forced him to list all his credentials –

and by listing them he hoped that people would accept his witness – he started by boasting of all the things he received, the advantages he had over those who called his mission in question. At the end, however, he added that he would much rather boast of his weaknesses:

> Wherefore, so that I should not get above myself, I was given a thorn in the flesh, a messenger from Satan to batter me and prevent me from getting above myself. About this, I have three times pleaded with the Lord that it might leave me; but he has answered me. 'My grace is enough for you: for power is at full stretch in weakness.' It is, then, about my weaknesses that I am happiest of all to boast, so that the power of Christ may rest upon me; and that is why I am glad of weaknesses, insults, constraints, persecutions and distress for Christ's sake. For it is when I am weak that I am strong. (2 Cor. 12:7–10 NJB).

We may safely leave unresolved the question as to the kind of 'messenger of Satan' that troubled Paul. The text makes clear that Paul had to contend with some form of temptation, one in which he was poignantly confronted with his own weakness. It was so bad that Paul took refuge in prayer and begged the Lord to remove this temptation from him. We may wonder if perhaps Paul feared being weak; was that thought perhaps intolerable to him? But Jesus did not grant him his wish. The temptation was not removed from him – it was much more important that he should continue to be tested so that he might learn in his own experience where and how the omnipotence of God best comes into its own. Important here was not Paul's strength, or his personal victory over temptation, but only his continuing in it, and so continuing in grace. For grace does not connect with our strength or our virtue, but only with our weakness. Accordingly, it is amply sufficient; and therefore we are only strong enough when our weakness has been demonstrated with perfect clarity. For it is precisely the place where the surprise of the grace of Jesus comes over us.

Being reconciled with one's weakness

This fact about our weakness is not immediately obvious in the daily experience of one's spiritual life. Most of us become uneasy, even desperate sometimes, the moment we are rudely made aware of our weakness. Some of us take to our heels. In order to remain in our weakness, to become reconciled with one's sinfulness, a person needs in fact to have some experience of the love of God. The big temptation, then, consists in attempting to fool ourselves into believing that that weakness is really not ours at all. Some of us even manage to deny the presence of any trace of weakness in ourselves. That is very bad. The life of such people may, because of their intense efforts, then be called 'beautiful' or 'noble'; nevertheless, it will remain compulsive and rigid, a life in which real love cannot well up. They are on the brink of becoming hardened and close to spiritual blindness.

Fortunately, this is not usually the case. We do know our weakness, thank God, but we do not know what to do with it. It is not consistent with the ideal self-image we unconsciously carry everywhere with us. After all, we naturally imagine that holiness is to be found somewhere beyond sin, and we count on God to demonstrate his love to us by keeping us from weakness and sin in order thus to make our holiness possible. But that is not how God operates. Holiness does not lie on the other side of temptation; it is to be found in the midst of temptation. It does not sit waiting for us on a level above our weakness; it is given us in weakness, or else we would elude the power of God that is operative only in our weakness. Rather we must learn to 'abide' in weakness, and to do so full of faith, open to the weakness and in utter surrender to God's mercy. It is only in our weakness that we are vulnerable to his love and power. Accordingly, to continue in the situation of temptation and weakness is the only way for us to connect with grace, the only way we can become miracles of God's mercy.

This is what happened to Peter. Hardly had he denied his Master for the third time when 'the Lord turned and looked at Peter. Then Peter remembered the word of the Lord, how he had said to him, "Before the cock crows today, you will

deny me three times." And he went out and wept bitterly'
(Luke 22:61–2 NRSV). We can only guess what that look meant
to Peter, but it was certainly not one of condemnation. 'For
I came not to judge the world but to save it,' Jesus himself
had said (John 12:47). Nor was it a look of correction. It was
a look of generous, warm, caring love. 'Merciful Lord, gra-
cious God, infinitely patient love . . . As a father has compassion for his children, so he has compassion for us as a
merciful Father' (Ps. 103:13). It occurred at precisely the
moment Peter realized that he had disowned Jesus and felt
himself to be a traitor. It was *then* that Jesus' loving look hit
and hurt him and in the same moment granted him forgiveness in love. Not only did Jesus grant forgiveness; he also
summoned Peter to a new life. At one stroke Peter became
another person. His mood collapsed; his heart melted. Now
he knew the reality of love. 'But God proves his love for us
in that while we were still sinners Christ died for us' (Rom.
5:8 NRSV). Peter broke down in tears, a clear sign of the wound
that Jesus' look caused in him. He wept bitter tears, Luke
remarks; and no doubt that was the impression made on an
outsider who only saw Peter weeping from a distance. But we
may also assume that deep inside Peter's heart they were tears
of joy and of gratitude because by that loving glance Jesus
did not abandon him to his pain and despair but, in his very
own person and on the spot, gave him a fresh sign of love.

It would not be the last time Jesus' look would confuse and
upset Peter in a healing way. The most poignant instance of
this would take place on the Easter day itself. The gospels
have left us no details of the personal encounter between
Peter and the newly risen Jesus. But they have left a crisply
formulated witness that continues ever after as perhaps the
most ancient proclamation or *kerygma* of the resurrection: 'The
Lord has risen indeed, and he has appeared to Simon!' (Luke
24:34). Paul too, in his list of the appearances of the risen
Jesus, inserted the appearance to Peter at the top of the list:
'. . . that he was buried, that he was raised on the third day
in accordance with the scriptures, and that he appeared to
Cephas and then to the twelve' (1 Cor. 15:4–5). Other witnesses tell us that Jesus first appeared to Mary Magdalene
(Mark 16:9), then to the two disciples 'as they were walking

into the country' (Mark 16:12). It was these two, better known, thanks to Luke's story, as the two disciples of Emmaus (Luke 24:13–35), who returned that same Easter evening to Jerusalem to learn from the apostles the good news that Jesus had already appeared to Peter.

Jesus' appearance must have greatly shocked Peter, who perhaps still lived in strong awareness of his cowardly denial a couple of days before. Not only was Jesus for him, as for the other disciples, dead and buried, but somewhere in his mind he felt also that he was an accomplice in causing that death. Far from staying with Jesus until death, as he had so rashly and recklessly promised beforehand, he had abandoned Jesus at the most critical moment. Then, early on Easter morning, there had been some mention of an empty grave. Peter together with John had run to it to check, and indeed the Lord's body had disappeared and no one had even a suspicion who had done it or where the body had been taken. All this upset him still more. Then suddenly it happened – the same warm voice, the same love-filled look. Peter forgiven in a flash and forever, healed of his deepest weakness and at the same time restored . . . And again the tears, doubtless more than ever tears of joy and gratitude. For Jesus so loved Peter that he searched him out even in his denial and betrayal and wanted to meet him intimately. On that radiant Easter morning Peter was the very first sinner to be forgiven and to repent.

The climax of this adventure was reserved by John the evangelist for the end of his gospel. This is the intimate and moving scene where Jesus three times asked Peter if he loved him more than he loved the others. And three times Peter declared his love for him, just as three times he had denied him: 'Lord, you know everything; you know that I love you' (John 21:15–17). It is clear that Peter, like another sinner elsewhere in the gospel, now loved much more than ever before because he too had been forgiven much (Luke 7:47). Jesus immediately drew the conclusion: 'Feed my sheep'. For one who had experienced so much love and mercy could also be first and best at bearing witness to that love: 'Once you have turned back, strengthen your brothers' (Luke 22:32).

5

BETWEEN WEAKNESS AND GRACE

THE TITLE OF this chapter was at first 'Virtue and Grace'. It was only later that I realized this might give rise to misunderstanding. Without wanting to recommend the opposite of virtue, which is vice, it seems to me risky to speak about the virtue that connects with God's work of grace in us.

The reason is that there are different ways of applying oneself to virtue, ways that are sometimes mutually exclusive. To put it plainly, there is a sort of virtuousness that cannot connect with grace; there is another kind that can flow only from grace. It is therefore important to define clearly the distinction between the two; otherwise the business of dealing with, and appealing to, virtue runs into serious objections. I finally opted for the title 'Between Weakness and Grace' because, as will be evident from what follows, evangelical virtue has as much to do with weakness as with grace.

Evangelical virtue?

The Greek equivalent for virtue (*aretè*) is not part of Jesus' vocabulary and occurs very seldom in the New Testament (Phil. 4:8; 2 Pet. 1:5). The believing disciple of Jesus is called not so much to virtue as to holiness, but this is a holiness that is not his own but available only in Jesus. Of course, this does not alter the fact that all who have wanted to speak about the Christian experience had a lot to say about virtue and perfection. Outsiders have from time to time even considered Christians above all as virtuous people. This is hardly surprising. In order to say anything about the experience of faith and of grace a speaker or writer is dependent on current patterns of perfection and vocabulary.

But such a person must not fall a victim to that vocabulary. It is always difficult to speak of spiritual experience in human terms. Even so, though human terms remain inadequate, the Church has to speak out, as in fact it has done for centuries. Accordingly, when spiritual writers speak of growth in the life of grace, they readily use expressions like 'advancing', 'making progress', 'climbing higher'. In using these expressions they are leaning on what we may call philosophical or humanistic patterns of perfection. The great thinkers of world literature as a rule conceived human perfection in the form of steady progression, a more or less perilous ascent, totally the fruit of human effort. And if perfection implies a certain self-discipline, the technique of that self-discipline is designed by human beings themselves and lies within reach of their own noble impulses. The assumption is that, when people reach the finishing line of the ascent, their effort automatically leads into glorious freedom – a freedom they themselves have paid for dearly.

It is important for us to realize clearly that such a model of perfection follows a route that is the precise opposite of that which confronts us in the gospels. Jesus himself, in a statement that appears regularly in varying contexts, tersely but very firmly indicates this contrast: 'Anyone who raises himself up will be humbled, and anyone who humbles himself will be raised up' (Matt. 23:12; Luke 14:11; 18:14 NJB). It is also these two models of spiritual effort which he doubtlessly sought to depict in the parable of the Pharisee and the publican, where these two are seen together in the temple. The Pharisee represented the model of a natural, ultimately humanistic and secularized perfection; the publican represented the specifically Christian way, the way of repentance, which humans can never discover by themselves but to which they are brought by God himself as the fruit of an undeserved election and as a miracle of grace.

There is a danger of contamination between the two ways. To describe their own unique experience Christians can never dispense with the terminology of humanistic perfection, the only diction available to them. Even when Christian authors do their best to purge the meaning of these words and, so to speak, reverse their direction, they will at times not be able to avoid appearing to adopt the humanistic model. Spiritual authors are virtually forced to use words and images like 'progress' and 'ascent'. They have to speak of 'degrees', 'steps', 'mountain', and 'summit'. Their vocabulary is in such great danger of being misunderstood that the contrast between the Pharisee and the publican recurs throughout the history of Christian and monastic spirituality. Nor is this surprising. For what emerges here is an essential tension that not only inheres in the words used but reflects a natural tendency of the human heart – perhaps the most treacherous temptation for those who are most sincerely in quest of God. That temptation can only be overcome by continuing conversion in the heart.

The most ancient church authors employed similar images, which in fact they derived from the Bible. People climb Mount Sinai right up to the cloud in which the Lord dwells, or Mount Carmel where the prophet Elijah was favoured with a vision of God, or Mount Zion where the Lord had his temple built, and especially Mount Tabor where Jesus was transfigured and so revealed himself to his disciples. The image of the ladder also served the idea of climbing up. The ladder that Jacob saw in his dream and that linked earth with heaven was employed by ancient authors as a description of progress in the spiritual life. This ladder had various rungs on which one could bravely practise the ascent. Thus in the sixth century a certain John, nicknamed Climacus (i.e. of the Ladder), described the whole monastic life in terms of mounting a ladder that had no fewer than thirty-three rungs. Benedictus in his Rule – we shall return to that later – knew a ladder of humility that was limited to twelve steps.

These images are appealing. They may convey the impression that the whole point is to make progress and to climb ever higher. *Excelsior!* We need to be careful, however, in choosing the ladder on which we start out. For there are countless unfit ladders, those of purely human virtue or goodness. There is only one good one, the ladder of humiliation. Saint Benedict seems to have been totally conscious of the ambivalence inherent in the word 'steps' when he used it to indicate progression in humility. To ensure clarity he immediately added that one climbs by going down, and that one goes down the moment one sets out to rise above it; that one must descend to rise and ascend by going down: *'exaltatione descendere et humilitate ascendere'*. The top rung of that ladder is the height of humiliation; and the elevation it may afford in the future can only be reached by flying low in this life. For that matter, no one can set out on this road, except by invitation from God. Only a divine vocation (*vocatio divina*) can devise the rungs in the ladder and ensure that one can rise by means of them. For the Christian there is no other way and no other virtue except that of descent toward one's littleness and insignificance. But still the temptation to a legalistic perfection constantly crops up. Especially in periods of spiritual decline there is a great danger that certain forms of committed faith – for example, the monastic life and all forms of militancy – will be seriously infected by it, although one does not immediately realize that a basic change of direction has occurred. Obedience, self-discipline, even prayer – these can all be directed away from the living God and become subordinated to an ideal of perfection that in essence barely differs from a secular ethic. It then turns into merely human effort, a fortress into which one retreats in order to have a position of strength in relation to others and sometimes even in relation to God. If in such a system of righteousness there is still room for repentance, it becomes just one more exercise among many. But then repentance is no longer the miracle of grace that transforms a human being from tip to toe, the threshold one must cross in order to start a new existence and to become totally free and open to the magnetism of the Holy Spirit.

This evidently was the kind of monastic life that Luther – with precious little success – had sought to realize, and whose image he, unfortunately and unfairly, was to represent at the very moment he had to pay for his experience with complete failure. 'Monasticism', wrote Dietrich Bonhoeffer,

> had transformed the humble work of discipleship into the meritorious activity of the saints, and the self-renunciation of discipleship into the flagrant spiritual self-

assertion of the 'religious'. The world had crept into the very heart of the monastic life, and was once more making havoc. The monk's attempt to flee from the world turned out to be a subtle form of love for the world. The bottom having thus been knocked out of the religious life, Luther laid hold upon grace. Just as the whole world of monasticism was crashing about him in ruins, he saw God in Christ stretching forth his hand to save. He grasped that hand in faith, believing that 'after all, nothing we can do is of any avail, however good a life we live.*

These words of Bonhoeffer contain a real challenge to any form of committed faith whatever. They expose a monasticism said to have become merely ordinary human effort, directed against God. The spectre of such monasticism is not just a caricature. It remains always a potential danger and is perhaps the most treacherous temptation of our time. Could it be any different for a monasticism that would see itself secularized right down to its very essence? Only the experience of repentance can separate monasticism from such outward show and be its salvation. For only by experiencing repentance intensely can a monk discover and realize from within how far true ascesis (spiritual self-discipline) and experience of God lie outside the reach of man and are not the result of one's own exertions. They are exclusively *opus Dei*, a work of God, in a heart that is completely surrendered to its own misery and the overwhelming compassion of God.

If in the gospels we want to find anew some sense of that ambiguity and that tension which has existed throughout the centuries, we come again to the extraordinarily beautiful parable of the Pharisee and the publican (Luke 18:9–14).

Pharisee or publican?

This parable deals with the good and the bad ladder, with genuine virtue and pseudo-virtue, and also with genuine and misguided thanksgiving. The Pharisee, having taken a con-

*Dietrich Bonhoeffer, *The Cost of Discipleship*, Macmillan, 1963, p. 50; *Nachfolge*, Kaiser Verlag, 1937.

spicuous place in the temple, uttered a solemn prayer of thanksgiving totally in the style of the official prayers of thanksgiving current at the time: 'God, I thank you . . . !' But he thanked God for his own virtue. He thought he was superior to the others, to thieves, rogues, adulterers, and especially 'that publican over there'. The Pharisee placed himself conspicuously at the top of the ladder and congratulated God on what he thought was genuine virtue in himself. A person may stand on the same ladder, putting himself or herself a few or several rungs below that of the Pharisee, but still be on the wrong ladder. This happens, for example, when our assessment of our spiritual poverty and cowardice throws us, like the Pharisee, back upon ourselves and causes all sorts of negative feelings to well up in ourselves: discontent, discouragement, envy, even despair perhaps. We then envy others for what we consider their virtue and we are inconsolable over our own mediocrity. All those feelings, being contented or discontented, condemning others or envying them, are a sign that we are on the wrong ladder, the ladder of the Pharisee, and that we are looking in the wrong direction.

Because the Pharisee in the parable was totally focused on his own virtue, when he caught sight of the publican as he was praying, he immediately saw a chance to write him off. The publican, however, made no comparison; he did not seem to see the Pharisee or hear his prayer. He had eyes only for God, and for himself only to the degree that he saw himself in God's light; he was a sinner. But he was not totally crushed by his sin, for he remembered his sin only to the extent that he could bare it to God's mercy: 'God, be merciful to me a sinner.' Making progress, climbing higher – none of this occurs to the publican. On the contrary, in God's light his smallness was enough for him. That was *his* deep truth, one that enabled him to stand naked, without masks, before the face of God. He might even explore and fathom that truth further, but always in terms of the marvellous power of God's compassion. This made him content and happy. Involuntarily one recalls expressions used by some sixteenth- and seventeenth-century mystics: to 'an-nihil-ate' oneself, that is, to grow attached to one's own insignificance and nullity and 'abide' in it. The prayer of the publican was that he might abide in his nothingness, to attach himself as it were to his weakness and sin that God might be God in him. In that way he could be totally himself – nothing, a sinner. And God could be totally himself with him – mercy, overwhelming love. The publican was standing on the right ladder and was moving in the right direction: *humiliando ascendit*, by going down he was climbing up.

The Pharisee and the publican, the two people Luke contrasts with each other, represent two human types, two spiritual postures, that regularly recur in Jesus' teaching. On the one side, Pharisees, Sadducees and scribes, examples of official virtuousness; on the other, publicans, Samaritans, prostitutes – in a word, sinners. Two types of human-beings who live in tension with and in opposition to each other. Jesus did little to bring them together. On the contrary, one gets the impression that he deliberately heightened the tension between the two. In the end the Pharisees got angry because he spent too much time with sinners and publicans, a charge that kept coming up in discussions between them and Jesus. Anyway, Jesus was exceptionally hard and severe with the one group and at the same time unaccountably good and lenient with the other. Speaking of Pharisees Jesus just about exhausted the vocabulary of invective; to him they were hypocrites (Matt. 23:13), snakes, brood of vipers (Matt. 23:33), whitewashed tombs one could walk past without seeing them, beautiful on the outside and full of corruption inside (Matt. 23:27), blind guides of the blind (Matt. 15:14) seemingly righteous to others but inside full of hypocrisy and lawlessness (Matt. 23:28). But Jesus' main grievance was that they 'trusted in themselves that they were righteous' (Luke 18:9); they belonged, not among sinners, but to a special class of people on whom they thought God showered his attention. This was precisely where the misunderstanding lay. Jesus came not for the righteous but for sinners (Matt. 9:13), and those who do not recognize how they belong in the category of sinners cannot connect with Jesus. It is the sinners and prostitutes, after all, who precede others into the kingdom of God (Matt. 21:31).

When Jesus so vehemently attacked the Pharisees it was because in them he encountered real sin. Sin is not always to be found where people generally look for it and label it as such. This becomes clear in another dispute Jesus had with Pharisees (John 9), just after the healing of the man born blind. It was not the man blind from birth who was *really* blind, said Jesus, for he would gain his sight. But those who claimed to see, as the Pharisees did, who were blind, and that permanently.

It was the Pharisees who linked the man's blindness with sin: 'Rabbi, who sinned, this man or his parents, that he should have been born blind?' (John 9:2).* It is striking in the story how ready the Pharisees were to connect everybody with sin. The blind man was said to be guilty because he had been born blind. Jesus was called a sinner because he accomplished a healing on the Sabbath. The bystanders were suspect because they did not know the Law (John 7:49). It is clear, therefore, that without a second thought the Pharisees ranked themselves among the righteous and despised others. *They* knew the Law but the people running after the rabbi did not. *They* knew that this man Jesus could not be from God, because God does not listen to sinners who violate the Sabbath. And whatever could they learn from a person who had just been healed of his blindness! ' "You, a sinner through and through, you want to teach us?" Then they threw him out' (John 9:34).

Thus the Pharisees were inaccessible to Jesus. Jesus was simply blocked by them, and as a result could not do anything for them. They lived in the isolated ivory towers of their own self-sufficiency and self-righteousness. For Jesus did not come for people who can see well; he came for the blind. He searches out *sinners*, who therefore have the first and best chance of entering the Kingdom that is near. To carry out his task as Saviour he needs sin and blindness. This is the judgement he preached, the judgement for which he came – that they who come to know their sin are healed and restored, and that they who cover up their sin and proceed to forget it will not be able to escape being judged in the end. Jesus, linking his words with the healing of the man blind from birth, put it

*It was actually Jesus' disciples who asked the question. Its import, however, was Pharisaic. *Translator.*

this way: 'It is for judgement that I have come into this world, so that those without sight may see and those with sight may become blind' (John 9:39).

It could not have been put more paradoxically, and the Pharisees understood that the point of the paradox was aimed straight at them: 'Some Pharisees who were present, said to him, "So we are blind, are we?" Jesus replied, "If you were blind, you would not be guilty, but since you say, "We can see," your guilt remains' (John 9:40). This is clear, the real sin consists in their saying that they are not blind. Being blind would not be so bad. One who is blind is open to being healed. But their sin is that they think and say they can see.

The Good News

The Good News of Jesus is first and foremost that we are sinners and that our sin has been forgiven. Sometimes people have the idea that the Good News is rather that we should beware of sin and do our best not to fall into it; that, accordingly, it is good to know where sin begins and where sin ends. The first object of the Good News is not the identification of what is sin and what is not sin. That would be the Good News of the Pharisees, not of Jesus. On the contrary, the Good News of Jesus is that our sin, whatever it may be, has been forgiven. Therefore our great joy is that we are forgiven sinners – the only assurance left to us in the world before God and a source of everlasting gratitude. The grace Jesus would give us is that we begin to suspect – barely begin and barely suspect – that we are sinners. That is the sign that at last our eyes are opening and that we are at the point of being healed of our blindness, the clear sign of grace. That is our only joy on earth and also the only joy in heaven: 'There will be more joy in heaven over one sinner who repents than over ninety-nine righteous persons who need no repentance' (Luke 15:7).

Only by this route may we at some time hope to be the joy of God. God has so willed it that he would manifest his love through the experience of sin and grace. Paul pithily expresses this in two of his letters: 'For God has imprisoned all in disobedience so that he may be merciful to all' (Rom. 11:32); and 'But the scripture has imprisoned all things under the power of sin' (Gal. 3:22). To be caught up in sin in order to be caught in the net of God's mercy: that is the only road that leads to God, rather, the only road on which God daily runs out to meet us, the way of *felix culpa*, the blessed fault, the fault that is our best chance because it discloses the grace of God to us.

The sinner is therefore not an unfamiliar figure to God. Quite the opposite, God only wants to know the sinner. And the sinner is also the only human being who in due course gets to know something about God. Graham Greene, the British novelist of whom it was said that the only theme he treated in his novels was that of the contemplative sinner, inscribed the title page of one of his novels with these words of Péguy: 'The sinner is at the very heart of Christianity. No one is as competent to speak on the subject of Christianity as the sinner. No one, except the saint . . .' Thus at some point there is no longer any difference between the sinner and the saint. For the saint is merely, and above all, a repentant sinner.

In the course of this book we shall, in various ways and from different angles, consider this road of sin and mercy. It is the obvious place from which we may connect with God and learn to attune ourselves to his marvellous grace. This response lies forever embodied in the publican's brief ejaculatory prayer. In a certain tradition, in the form of the well known Jesus Prayer, it has developed into virtually the only prayer formula: 'Lord, be merciful to me, a poor sinner!' Jesus himself says of this prayer that it includes forgiveness and justification in the sense of sanctification; it was the publican who went to his home justified rather than the other. 'For all who exalt themselves will be humbled but all who humble themselves will be exalted' (Luke 18:14).

For the monk who, in the words of Benedict, has reached the topmost rung of the ladder of humility, the publican's prayer has also become the only prayer, the unending internal liturgy which the monk celebrates wherever he goes or stands, sitting or walking, not daring to raise his eyes to heaven but constantly repeating the same prayer in his heart: 'Lord, be merciful to me a sinner!' (*The Rule of St Benedict*, chapter 7).

In this prayer East and West meet each other, for it is as

familiar to Byzantine as to Latin monks. It is perhaps the heart, the inmost ground, of the Church. I recall a visit to a hermitage in the north of Moldavia, close to the Romanian border. The dwelling belonged to the Sikla *skyt* (small, secluded monastery), itself part of the Sihastria monastery, which is occupied to this day by a little under a hundred monks. The monastery is located in a region that has for centuries been inhabited only by monks, a kind of Romanian Athos. The *skyt* lies hidden somewhere in the forests at an elevation of more than a thousand metres. A little further up, under a high, sheer cliff, stood the hermitage. On its door an unsteady hand had inscribed the prayer of the publican: 'Lord Jesus, be merciful to me, a poor sinner!' That short prayer had apparently become the hermit's motto, his life motto as it were, his cry in the heart of the Church. It is the cry that makes the Church into the Church, the bride of Jesus; the cry that is the epitome of all prayer. Beyond this cry there is really no more prayer, but only love, the embrace between the Father and the prodigal son, between Jesus and the publican, the long awaited connection between the abyss of our sin and the abyss of God's mercy.

6

CONTRITION OF THE HEART

TO MANY READERS the title of this chapter will seem strange and old-fashioned. The more informed readers may think I should have used the more usual modern synonym, 'repentance'. And it is true that 'contrition of heart' is one of the old expressions regularly used to describe repentance. It is the literal translation of the Latin expression *contritio cordis* which the Fathers often used together with the word *compunctio*.

The advantage of these two old terms is twofold. In the first place they are not as threadbare as the word 'repentance'. Secondly, the terms are quite graphic, conveying accurately what happens to us in a well-defined and very important spiritual experience. They are images which can tell us more than an abstract definition.

Contritio (literally, 'crushing') conveys the idea clearly. Something is broken, shattered, in our inmost being. Our stony hearts, as the Bible calls them, are no more. Something gives in, or gives up. The heart gives way to brokenness; soon we have only the pieces left.

Compunctio is equally suggestive. It is derived from the verb 'to prick' or 'pierce'. At some moment our heart is decisively injured, is pierced. From that wound in the heart, says the tradition, water will well up – the tears of repentance.

It is safer perhaps, if it is our intention to talk about repentance, to start with those two old images. For in today's world the subject of repentance has become a difficult one, a problem it shares with the word 'humility'. Both words arouse resistance and distrust. What kind of repentance and what kind of humility are we talking about? That is an extremely subtle question, one that cannot easily be answered. The difficulty is not just that it is always risky to approach a typically spiritual experience like repentance intellectually and from the outside. That difficulty is perennial. In our own time, however, the question has become even more complex, for two reasons.

On the one hand, until a couple of decades ago, areas of moral effort, including the active and contemplative religious life, were dominated by guilt feelings accompanied by *angst* and psychological defence mechanisms arising from these. On the other hand, in today's world people often resist openly all inner and outer pressure. This has led them, in reaction to that *angst*, to a complete reversal of behaviour in order to regain their freedom, often taking the form of a looseness of morality from which the aspect of sin has totally disappeared. Just as a young person plunges into a semblance of freedom to escape his *angst* without having taken time to pay the price for that freedom or by waiting to become more mature, so many modern people, including Christians and monastics, are equally ill prepared to see the tender flower of evangelical repentance unfold in their hearts. If by chance, in the grace of God, it does begin to bloom there, they have the greatest difficulty in identifying and appreciating it.

The discernment (*diakrisis*) needed here is particularly difficult. It can emerge only under the continual action of the Holy Spirit on our personal subconscious where true repentance tends to get bogged down. Spiritual authors have at all times warned, for example, against *false* humility, the tendency to seek self-humiliation which, according to Fénelon, is often proof of veiled pride. This kind of humility is a clumsy expression of an indefinite feeling of guilt, but it does not leave in the heart a single trace of genuine humility. False humility tends rather to impose restraints on the heart and paralyse it because, with all the tricks at its disposal, it causes one to evade the truth that could trigger the awareness of one's real sin. But these days, the reaction to this guilt feeling is often to adopt a sort of false freedom which crowds out the confrontation with sin and represses any upsurge of repentance. In both cases the unconscious attempt is to the same purpose – to escape the feeling of falling short and of being a sinner.

The alternative to false guilt and false freedom can only be overcome in genuine evangelical repentance, that is, in the brokenness of heart that is purely a gift of the Holy Spirit. Through that process alone a person may arrive at full truth in his or her relationship to God and, in the end, to genuine love; for love alone is the fountain of true freedom.

Guilt and repentance

> One who knows his sins is greater than he who raises a corpse to life. One who weeps over himself for an entire hour is greater than he who furnishes information to the whole world . . . One who knows his weakness is greater than he who sees the angels . . . The solitary and repentant follower of Christ is greater than he who enjoys popular favour in the churches.

By these paradoxes Saint Isaac the Syrian put his finger on the specifically Christian character of repentance (Logos no. 34).

This is something that needs to be stated clearly. You will encounter really liberating repentance nowhere else, and in no other religion, than in the Christian gospel. Christian repentance cannot be subsumed under, or compared with, any other experience derived from natural religions. Any attempt to copy or imitate someone else's repentance will immediately turn ludicrous or lead to psychic imbalance. Repentance is a fruit of the Holy Spirit and one of the most trustworthy indications of his operation in the soul.

No one can get to know his or her sin without at the same time getting to know God – not before or afterwards, but simultaneously in one and the same moment of spiritual insight.

Anyone who thinks he knows his sin apart from the encounter with God still lives in a state of illusion. He confuses repentance with a more or less developed feeling of guilt that lies within the experience of every normal human being. Or he reads his sin from a list of obligations or commandments with which his conduct is more or less in harmony. But his real sin he does not know because he does not yet know God.

At the very moment that the sinner receives forgiveness and is caught up by God and restored in grace, at that moment – wonder of wonders! – sin has become the place where God enters into contact with a human being. One even may go further and say that there is no other way to encounter God and to learn to know him than by the way of repentance. Before then God was only a word, a concept, a premonition, a vague longing, the God of philosophers and poets but not yet the God who reveals himself in unfathomable love. For the Lord came to call sinners, to stay with them and to eat with them, not with the righteous; he came to seek that which was lost (Matt. 9:13; Luke 19:10). Thus God makes himself known by forgiving. And the sinner, by plumbing the depths of his sin, will discover the space of God's mercy at the very moment that the one swallows up the other.

This moment of grace is the primary and most fundamental part of a real encounter with the gospel. It is the experience of the 'little ones', the poor in spirit, and especially of conspicuous sinners, women of the street and publicans, the people who precede others into the kingdom of God (Matt. 21:31). It is in them and in the likes of them that God decided to meet and to save mankind. There is no other situation in which God so personally presents himself and brings salvation.

In this moment of grace both sin and forgiveness disclose themselves. Outside of this experience one can gain only fragmentary knowledge of God and humanity. One attains only half-truths, part-truths, which as alternatives seem to exclude each other. In human-beings one encounters acts of unfaithfulness that accumulate and at last become either a crushing weight or a display of virtue by which they pretend to be better than they are. Are they sinners or righteous? On the side of God one hesitates between his power and his tenderness, his wrath and his love. Is he the God of power or of tenderness? Of wrath or of love? Both attributes are shown in the Bible. They seem contradictory but only to one's intellect, and therefore the contradiction cannot be transcended by those who consider these questions only with their intellect. Only for those who personally and existentially experience the tenderness of God who forgives them their sins do the two

And again, Job's "sins" seem to be more along the lines of the inherent human shortcomings of great ignorance, a angel —

CONTRITION OF THE HEART   63

coincide. Then, without being able to explain this reality, they know intuitively that God is simultaneously Wrath and Love, or in the words of Scripture, Truth and Mercy. No one can experience being the object of God's wrath without at the same time sensing that this is a necessity for his love. No one will ever at any time find rest in God's love without being reminded that God's jealousy may at any moment ignite into wrath. God is no capricious despot, but neither is he an overly benevolent grandfather type. He is simply different. He cannot be caught in these concepts and images; he is mysterious and contradictory far above our shallow penetration. His mystery can only be grasped – and that only on a very modest scale and progressively – by those to whom it is given to meet God in conversion and in love.

Conversion, as we have seen earlier in this book, is a reversal, an about-face of the heart. It denotes a spiritual process in our inmost being by which our heart is liberated from rigidity and compulsiveness, abandons all self-will and ambitions, detaches itself from itself in order to surrender itself to God, and is simultaneously the object of his wrath and his love. The heart that thus yields to God finds that the spark of God's wrath changes in a flash into a blaze of love and tenderness. Then God in truth becomes a devouring fire (Deut. 4:24).

Only those who thus continue in their conversion truly know God. For they know their sin. Though they are confronted by the wrath of God, at the same time they discern the greatness and superior strength of God's love. They will never cease to acknowledge their sin, in order in that way to proclaim God's mercy. Their acknowledgement is not only an act of confession but also an act of thanksgiving; it becomes eucharistic in nature. Their tears are tears no longer of sorrow but of a warm love. Their repentance is their joy; their only joy is now their repentance. They have given credence to love; they have surrendered themselves to love (cf. 1 John 4:16), to Jesus who 'rescues us from the wrath that is coming' (1 Thess. 1:10).

The monk and the publican

Perhaps at this point someone will object that this experience is granted to and reserved for real sinners, that is to say, those who had a lot to answer for before they met Jesus; so what about committed Christians who as a rule have only peccadilloes on their conscience and for the rest live exemplary lives? This objection suggests that we still divide Jesus' followers into 'sinners' and 'righteous', and tend instinctively to rank ourselves among the righteous.

This is precisely the attitude from which God seeks constantly to cure us. There is not one of us to whom sin, and, at the same time, God's mercy do not have to be revealed. No one is excluded, and especially not those who want to follow in Jesus' footprints, the committed, actively involved believer or the monk. In the ancient Syrian monastic tradition the monk was often given the name *abîla*, that is, a doleful one, one who grieves over his sin. And also in the Rule of Saint Benedict, which set a pattern for Western monasticism, the monk was characterized by repentance and contriteness of heart. We will pause a moment now to look into this phenomenon.

In the prologue of his Rule Benedict sets his pupil between God's wrath and God's love, between the *iratus Pater* (angry Father) and the *pius Pater* (merciful Father): a pair of alternatives the monk can bridge only by positioning himself in the humility of the conversion that will make him receptive to forgiveness from his Father. In order to perform this miracle God shows himself to be patient and merciful. He grants us the time of our present life by way of delay; it is a stratagem of his love. For God needs the course of our earthly life as the space in which he can unfold his mercy.

That mercy reaches its greatest potential only because of the patience and generosity of God – 'because he is merciful' (*quia pius est*). Each day he grants again deferment and in silence he yearns for us to apply our efforts and use our time to take the road back to him and to repent. The monk's response consists in humility, with all its nuances and degrees. Already the inner disposition, marked by St Benedict as the first step of that humility, determines the manner in which we must respond to that seeming weakness of God. If God grants delay, then the monk seeks to take advantage of the time given. He will shun forgetfulness of God. He pays careful attention and is on his guard. Internal vigilance, a careful weighing of his inclinations and longings, attention to his thoughts: these constitute a prologue to the purity of heart which, in St Benedict's account, as one reaches the utmost step of humility, puts the finishing touch on the image of the workman of God who from then on enjoys God's highest favour – 'now cleansed from vice and from sin'.

Thus the course of a monk's life runs exactly parallel with the Christian experience of repentance as we described it earlier. Here too Christian humility is paramount and at the heart of every associated inner experience. From the start of his monastic career humility is the touchstone of the young monk's calling. Even before the postulant is admitted he will have to face humiliations in order to test his zeal for humility (*The Rule*, ch. 58). Humility will then become the road on which the monastic life gradually develops. Even obedience, that especially highly esteemed 'work' of the monk, the road by which he goes toward God (ch. 71), is represented as a state of humility, the *primus humilitatis gradus* (the first step of humility), by which the relation between God and sinful man is reduced to its true proportion. All distinctions or hierarchy will be measured by or based on this fundamental grace. The preference of the abbot will be extended to the most humble (ch. 2), and the priests in the monastery must take special care to lead the other brothers by an example of greater humility (ch. 60). Finally, in order to describe the highest degree of the experience of humility, Benedict resorts to the classic image of the publican, perhaps the most evangelical image in existence. The humble and trusting acknowledgement of sin is to be seen not only in the prayer that wells up from an ever-flowing spring; soon it also expresses itself also in the monk's entire external bearing and conduct. Clearly the perfect monk is one who has the least status, both in his own eyes and those of others, but who never despairs of God's mercy. When, humanly speaking, he has descended to the lowest possible degree of earthly status and there is no longer any prospect for him – *incurvatus et humiliatus usquequaque* ('bowed down and humbled on every side') – he stands in closest proximity to God, propelled by an inexpressible urgency of tenderness and love. Here it is the same: there is no road by which God can be sought and reached other than the road of humility by which the heart, freed from the rigidity of self-love, is at a given moment turned unconditionally to grace and set on the conversion process that never ends.

Ascesis?

At this point the problem of ascesis (spiritual self-discipline) comes up. If we are solely dependent on God's mercy, what can we ourselves do about our condition? Does all exertion on our part then become fundamentally wrong? Our initial answer to this question can indeed be that any form of self-discipline that does not end in brokenness of heart would be of no value whatever. Even worse, instead of putting us on the track of God's grace it would tragically seal us off from it.

Ascesis has always been liable to misconception, and one therefore needs to be wary of it. It is important to return to the evangelical sources. The idea is not to give up on all spiritual effort or self-discipline but to learn to practise it only in ways which can connect us with the grace of God.

Our modern sensitivity may be helpful to us here. In general we are very conscious of the dubious features which characterized asceticism at certain periods of history. Ascetism may be confined to noble-minded activity. In that case it results in a Spartan or Nietzschian kind of rigidity where all available energy is expended on achieving an ideal that is only a more or less successfully noble form of human being. Asceticism of this kind will inevitably become the breeding ground of a well or poorly concealed pride. In any case the success attained would be very temporary. For the tension it evokes in the ascetic who practises it contrary to his true inner condition, undermines even the strongest psyche and is capable in a very short time of causing a general breakdown. No one can with impunity run ahead of the grace offered to him at any given moment. No one can practise ascesis in his or her own strength alone.

Another possibility of self-deception lies in an unhealthy craving for ascesis, which may compensate for an exaggerated sense of guilt and artificially serve to relieve the pressure unconsciously generated by the guilt. The balance of internal forces thus attained will remain very unstable. Worse, the problem is in no way cleared up by such effort, but continues to mask the real depths of the personality. Extreme self-discipline of this kind prevents the ascetic from making a complete self-surrender to the merciful love of God.

Where then can one find the ascesis that is specifically attuned to grace? Let us first make clear that it is normal for the body also to play a role in the adventure to which we are called. One cannot even speak of true spiritual passion apart from the body. My body is integral to my being. For the time being I will need a body to express life, and this holds true for even the most profound and spiritual aspects of that life. If we are to come to grips with true spiritual growth we need our body as much as our spiritual faculties. A genuine interior life can grow only through the body.

This is true of every system of spiritual development, inside or outside the Christian religion. Consequently, most of the classic forms of ascetic life are the same in virtually all religions and include poverty, silence, fasting, vigils. This integration of the body into the way of one's spiritual development is even more necessary when it concerns the spiritual fruits the Christian is called to bear. The primary reason is that the body as well as the spirit is marked by the congenital weakness the Bible calls sin. Baptism, though it brought us into a holy state, did not completely erase all the consequences of sin, from either our mind or our body. In both the traces of sin remain – a slippery slope in our inmost being by which we may easily slide toward sin. Therefore the body is also an area where grace must confront and counter sin. The Christian life must gradually take over the body by grace and again put it at the disposal of our basic spiritual freedom. Grace puts sin to death in our body; that is to say, it mortifies sin in us in order to make the body capable of transfiguration, transformation and glorification. All 'mortification' (the old word for ascesis) ought to lead to such transfiguration. In this way ascesis is rather like death. For the believer death is a

This also has a tinge of the belief that God cannot heal. There's always something wrong, God cannot fulfill bringing the Kingdom to Earth

prelude to the resurrection to new life in Jesus Christ which naturally and necessarily follows.

In speaking of ascesis we cannot evade this fundamental concept – death and resurrection in Jesus. Ascesis is simply our sharing in the paschal mystery of Jesus, a provisional and partial sharing in anticipation of the death that will fully incorporate us into the Easter-event. Every attempt at ascesis will take us deeper into this mystery and allow its power to open up a way into our body, which is gradually transformed into Christ's image and likeness. In order to bring about our salvation, Jesus took a body to himself. He became incarnate in this world of ours in order to confront the forces of sin and to triumph over them in his life and in his death. It is in the flesh, says St Paul, that Jesus has triumphed over sin (Eph. 2:14). Following the example of Jesus we also must put sin to death in our bodies, and thus allow the power of Christ's life, given to us in baptism, to triumph. True ascesis brings us into the mystery of Christ, and enables us to make progress in a very specific way in the life of Jesus, which could become manifest in us. In this sense every ascetic practice has an efficacy proper to itself.

It is true that all ascetic effort aims at bringing about the growth of the life of Christ in us, and this takes place in the deepest part of our being. But each individual practice is concerned with a particular area of that life, and this is important. Every ascetic sign possesses an efficacy which is proper to it, and which in a sense is naturally inherent in it. Thus we can speak of an ascesis which is natural to people and makes them fully human. For example, interior and exterior silence combined with solitude naturally favour recollection, and enable a person to concentrate on his or her interior world. It is also evident that night hours are more propitious to quiet and peaceful meditation, that fasting causes a hunger for spiritual things, and that celibacy creates an affective void which calls for fulfilment by profound and more universal love.

There exists a natural mysticism, the techniques of which are not all that different from those used by Christians. Those who engage in it testify to an interior wholeness which we do not always see in the life of the Christian. In so far as

Is this correct? Isn't the Kingdom at hand if we would only open our eyes?

CONTRITION OF THE HEART 69

technique, or the perfection of a particular means, is concerned, the natural mystics can often teach the believer something and help him in his search.

Yet we must say clearly that such ascesis, despite some good results, is not what Jesus Christ is seeking from his disciples. Only that ascetic effort which is the fruit of grace will truly promote the life of the Holy Spirit in their hearts. There is a fundamental disparity between all human effort, however perfect it may be, and the gift of grace which is given us in Jesus Christ. Grace is always freely given. This is the fundamental fact of all Christian experience, and so applies also to ascesis. Without the gift of grace ascesis is not Christian at all, but either pagan or simply a pastiche of ethics. God does not give himself according to the measure of our efforts. Jesus has not come for virtuous people but for sinners (Luke 5:32). He does not want what we call our virtues. He seeks our weakness so that his strength may grow in us without any limit, as St Paul tells the Corinthians (2 Cor. 12:9).

All ascetic effort therefore must be rooted in Jesus Christ. It must follow his example and imitate his life. The forms of ascesis which have been used spontaneously down the centuries are those which Christ used at one time or another during his earthly life. He was perfectly obedient in all things even unto death. The author of the Epistle to the Hebrews goes so far as to say that Jesus' body was given him in order to do God's will (Heb. 10:5–9). He always lived as a celibate. He had no place where he could lay his head (Luke 9:58). He undertook periods of intense fasting (Luke 4:2). He frequently retired into a desert place to spend the whole night in prayer (Mark 1:35; Luke 6:12).

The ascetic way of the Christian draws all its force from the power that Jesus placed in these very exercises by practising them during his earthly life. It is by contemplating Jesus that the Christian is able to re-create them in his own life. They are the ascetic exercises of Christ himself. And the Christian power to do them has been won for us by Christ, when he used these same practices in his own life to meet real temptation and trials and to overcome them once and for all.

The other point we must make is this. If any ascetic effort is to become truly Christian, it must be emptied of all its human power and potential and brought even to the point of failure, so that it can be taken over by the power of Christ. It is in our weakness and emptiness that the power of Christ is most active. Any ascesis that is truly evangelical is an ascesis of weakness and of poverty.

The ascesis of weakness

The aim of all ascetic effort is to make oneself nothing, and this nothingness is the closest we can come to God. It is a dying to self so as to be fully open to God. Our self-centredness is *the* obstacle to God's life and the action of his Spirit within us. By a strange paradox, the ascetic effort itself must share in this dying, this making ourselves to be nothing. It cannot achieve its goal of itself. At the precise point where our efforts fail, the power of God intervenes to bring our efforts to a perfection we cannot reach by our own power.

We are not talking here about some physical effort as though the ascetic could push his body as far as human capacity could go. We are talking about a moral nothingness, a self-effacement which is the bitter realization that the ascetic effort surpasses our strength and that God does not respond automatically as we had expected. God's grace is not to be measured by human effort.

This state of nothingness, this recognition of our own inadequacy, was called *acedia* by the ancient fathers. Known in English as 'accidie', it is *the* place of temptation for the monk. There he comes up against his own weakness and inadequacy and can even come up against despair.

Evagrius Ponticus, in particular, has given us an acute analysis of this crisis. Accidie is a state of extreme confusion in which the life of a monk is itself at issue. It can overpower everything, even blind the eyes of the heart (*Praktikos* 36) and 'dog-like, tears the soul to pieces as if it were a fawn' (*Praktikos* 23). It 'embraces almost all trials' (*Comm. on Ps. 139:3*). It attacks not the body but the soul; and not only a certain part of the soul, as concupiscence does for example, but 'is accustomed to embrace the entire soul and oppress the spirit' (*Praktikos* 36). In that sense accidie is not a local injury or passing crisis; it is an all-encompassing disease of the heart, *through everyone in an ultimate sense?*

a state of mind that penetrates and dooms to failure all it touches.

The danger of that state is that it grows increasingly more subtle. In an advanced stage accidie totally eludes the eyes of anyone who suffers from it; 'accidie darkens the divine light in one's eyes' (*Antirrhetikos* VI. 16). The confusion assumes increasingly virulent forms. Because of all his murmuring the monk forgets to sing and spoils his prayer. During the night vigil his tears dry up. The Rule loses all meaning and seems inhuman. The future is shut tight. 'What use is my life,' he thinks, 'it is hopeless'. Why did he ever become a monk? Did he not leave the world out of weakness or fear? Were his motives honest? In the city he could be much more useful, also to relatives and friends. Does God really ask for the demanding purity of heart held up as the ideal before his unsuspecting eyes as a novice? Is he not also content with the simple faith of those who live in the world? The truth is, God no longer answers any of these questions. Even his angels have abandoned him so that he is a prey to the devil. Nothing seems able to get him out of this dead-end feeling: 'Could even patience persuade God to have mercy on me?' (*Antirrhetikos* VI; 18).

In this way accidie brings the ascetic to his limits:

> The soul wastes away and suffers; it succumbs to the bitterness of *acedia*. Its powers collapse under the burden of this suffering. Its perseverance has been made to stagger under the violence of the mighty demon. It has lost its bearings and conducts itself as a small child that weeps tears of desperation and lies down hopelessly groaning for comfort. (*Antirrhetikos* VI: 38).

The reference to this relapse into childlike behaviour is significant. These symptoms, so unusual for a great ascetic, point to the danger of psychological regression. They show how deeply the spiritual life can be shaken by accidie. The monk has his back to the wall of his human limitations. He has reached the limits of his capacity to endure.

Sooner or later every way of ascesis comes more or less to this impasse. Accidie has turned into a sense of dizziness before the vast emptiness that lies between the soul and God, and the inability to get past it or even to bear it. Some accounts suggest that sometimes the ascetic is on the brink of becoming insane. It is to be expected that so powerful a trial as this, which calls all our habitual ways of acting into question, would bring us to the extremity of our weakness.

The question arises, what attitude should the ascetic assume in this crisis? The ancient fathers to whom Evagrius refers are unanimous in advising the ascetic to persevere, not to give up, not to leave his cell at any price. To which many a person will respond by asking, by what right can the ascetic in such a crisis be urged to persevere against all odds? The answer is simple, again according to Evagrius. The reason for this advice is that there is no shadow of doubt about what is coming. When his misery reaches rock-bottom, God's grace intervenes. Though at the end of his wits and energies, he does not despair: 'Be not be afraid and do not try to avoid this fruitful stage of your struggle. Be not afraid and you will see the great works of God: his assistance, his care, and all other forms of aid with a view to your salvation' (*Hypotyposis* VI). Someone who, out of love for Jesus, perseveres in solitude will see the demon of accidie succeeded by 'a state of deep peace and inexpressible joy' (*Praktikos* 12). One need only 'believe in God', 'to trust in him', 'to count on him', 'to persevere in trusting God', to remain 'quiet, alone, and still' in order not to lose God (*Antirrhetikos* VI 12, 14, 40, 41). The model is Job. His patient profile emerges from behind a number of admonitions: 'God wounds; he will also heal' (Job 5:17–19; cited in *Antirrhetikos* VI:31).

Evagrius perhaps owes this practical account of accidie to his spiritual father and teacher from the Egyptian desert, the renowned Macarius the Great. It was perhaps he who first used the term *contritio cordis*, the crushing of the heart, in a famous 'Letter to His Pupils', from which we will quote a few passages. In this letter Macarius describes how, though ascesis seems easy at first, the monk soon comes to feel that it lies totally beyond him:

> The monk gets to the point where it seems to him that he is totally unable to fast. He is at the point of succumb-

ing to his body because of his fatigue. Time seems endless. His thoughts tempt him: 'How long will you be able
to carry this enormous load?' Or, 'Could God possibly
forgive you that mountain of sins? . . .' Temptations
crowd in on him. In this condition the soul feels extremely
weak; the heart languishes to the point where the monk
comes to the conviction that celibacy is too much for
him. The temptations speak to him of a life that has to
go on forever, of virtue that is hard, of its heavy burdens
that are insupportable; also of his body that is so frail
and of human nature that is so weak . . . Under those
conditions the monk is comparable to a ship without a
helmsman that crashes into the rocks. His heart withers
and fails him. In every temptation he succumbs afresh.

Why should God permit the assault of such a merciless
crisis? It is the only way for him to break us open to his grace.
Macarius continues:

In this way in the end, the good God gradually opens
the eyes of his heart, so that he ends by understanding
that it is God alone who gives him strength. Only then
does man begin to give glory to God in the humility of
a contrite heart. As David says: 'Sacrifice to God is a
contrite heart' (Ps. 51:17). Indeed it is from such diffi-
culties in the struggle that humility, a contrite heart,
meekness and gentleness are born.

This text is one of the most ancient in all monastic literature, and it is enough by itself to counter any idea that ascesis
is some form of spiritual athletics, or that it is a matter of
physical prowess. Nothing could be more contrary to true
Christian ascesis. All Christian ascetic effort must bring about
a sort of heart-break; it must bring one to the point of nothingness of which we have spoken in order to make room for the
power and the grace of Jesus. Only in self-abasement and
humility can this happen, for grace is entirely beyond our
own efforts.

We do not speak, therefore, of ascetic prowess but of a true
miracle of grace. This is the only correct term when we talk

about the realization of Christian ascesis – celibacy, fasting, obedience and commitment. When a person learns from his, or her, own experience that the self-denial involved in these is something he cannot do of himself, then God gives him the grace. For us it is enough to give ourselves up to this miracle, to yield ourselves to it humbly in the joy of a broken heart, placing all our hope in the love of God.

We come back here to the original meaning of the word ascesis. We said that it means training, exercise, putting to the proof. But how does one exercise oneself in ascesis? What *is* this exercise we are talking about? It is not a question of exercising one's own strength in order to see how far one can go in ascesis. This matters little in Christian ascesis. It matters little to know whether or not you are capable of a particular ascetic practice. We must be borne along, not by our own strength but by God's grace. We must exercise ourselves in this grace and not in our own prowess or ability. We must know this grace truly and discern it correctly as it comes to us at each moment. If I am truly in touch with this grace, I can embark on the ascetic way without danger, for God calls me to it, and will not allow me to fail. But if I am out of touch with this grace, if I depend on myself, and am not borne up and carried by grace, if grace is not the motive force of my ascetic effort, then what right have I, as it were, to force God to intervene miraculously on my behalf? To do so would be both rash and foolhardy. To tune in to grace, to learn to act only out of grace is to be attentive at every moment to the interior impulse of the Spirit as he calls me in a particular direction.

As we proceed along the way of conformity with Jesus in the mystery of his death and resurrection, a certain measure of grace is given us at every moment. This measure is very exact, and we cannot presume on it. Likewise we must take care not to go beyond it. But neither ought we to underestimate it. Often we do not come up to the measure which God gives so generously and so bountifully. As Isaiah tells us, when it comes to miracles, 'The Lord's arm is not short' (59:1), and he is always ready to perform his wonders once again for his people.

Here a question arises: How do I come to discern with

any accuracy this measure of grace in myself? This question concerns the central problem in discerning of spirits. A beginner on the road of spiritual experience clearly cannot do it. In most cases, it is totally beyond him or her. This is the reason why tradition surrounds ascetic practices with so many conditions. Above all, however, tradition posits the necessity of a spiritual guide who is able to discern the movement of God's grace in us and who can over time help us to achieve a degree of proficiency ourselves. Nothing is easier than to misjudge the quality of interior impulses and inspirations, and to attribute to grace what is merely an illusion conjured up by our pride or egoism. To want to embark on an ascesis without being invited by clear signs of grace is to court failure; more than that, it is to tempt God. For that reason we shall return to the subject of spiritual guidance later on in this book.

The restored human being

A little earlier we heard Evagrius saying that accidie has to pass into 'a state of deep peace and inexpressible joy'. This is the state of human and spiritual completeness toward which we are ever in process of growing, the maturity of our full stature in Jesus Christ (cf. Eph. 4:13 NRSV). It is also called *apatheia* by Evagrius and the entire tradition of the Greek fathers. In the works of John Cassian it is occasionally called *integritas*, or wholeness. This last term seems to be the more apt. We are dealing, after all, not with a state in which human passions have been suspended but, on the contrary, with one in which they have recovered their original integrity and wholeness. It is the primal state of the soul, no longer damaged by passions that tear it apart. The powers and the longings of the soul which, initially disoriented by sin and in danger of collapsing or disintegrating under the violent impact of accidie, are again moving toward unity. A person can again be whole before God.

One must never forget, however, that this grace was granted at the low point of accidie and despair, at the moment when prayer could arise only from the depths, *de profundis*, of bottomless distress. In these circumstances prayer can exhibit only one's misery. It cries out for help and begs for forgiveness. But to the degree that the heart is inundated by prayer, it gradually finds peace and becomes reconciled with weakness and sin. Or rather, in the end it turns its eyes away from its own misery in order simply to contemplate the face of God's mercy. Repentance then passes unconsciously into modest, quiet joy, into a shy sort of love and giving of thanks. No false step or sin is denied or excused, but all are drowned in mercy. Where sin increased, there grace abounds all the more (cf. Rom 5:20). All that sin had ruined is restored by grace, much more beautiful than it was before. To be sure, prayer continues to bear the marks of sin and misery, perhaps for ever, but from here on we are dealing with a blessed fault, a *felix culpa*, as we say in our songs on Easter night, a guilt that is taken up and devoured by love. There is now hardly any difference between repentance and thanksgiving; the two merge into each other and the tears of repentance are no less tears of love.

Gradually this feeling of joyful repentance gains the upperhand in one's whole spiritual experience. Each day, from the ascesis of neediness, *patientia pauperum*, a new person arises. That person is the embodiment of peace, joy, kindness, gentleness. He or she remains for ever marked by repentance, a joyful, loving repentance that always and everywhere predominates and is continually in the background of that person's quest for God. He has now attained a deep serenity, for he was broken down and rebuilt from top to bottom, by pure grace. He barely recognizes himself; he has become another person. He had skirted the deep abyss of sin but simultaneously fallen into the abyss of God's mercy. He has now learned to put down his weapons before God, to be defenceless before him, and to hang on to nothing that would keep God at bay. He stands there naked and shattered. He has abandoned his virtue and no longer makes plans to attain holiness. His hands are empty, having nothing left but his own misery. But he dares to spread these out before the mercy of God. God has at last become really God for him. And only God, that is, *Salvator* – the Saviour from sin. He is almost reconciled with sin, just as God has reconciled himself with the person's sin. He is now grateful and happy because he has permission to be weak. He no longer needs to strive for perfection; that is but dirty linen in the sight of God (Isa. 64:6). His virtues? He possesses them only in God. Actually they are only his wounds, assuaged and healed by divine mercy, the wound having blossomed into wonder. Now he can but give thanks and praise to God, the God who is constantly at work within him and ever anew performs this miracle in his life.

To all his brothers and colleagues he has become a kind and gentle friend. Their defects no longer irritate him. He sympathizes with their weakness. His confidence is no longer in himself but in God. He is possessed, as it were, by the love and omnipotence of God. He is therefore also poor, really poor – poor in spirit – and stands close to all who are poor and to all forms of poverty, spiritual and physical. He regards himself as the foremost of sinners, but has obtained forgiveness. Therefore he can relate to all sinners in the world as an equal and a brother. He is close to them, because he is not better than they are. His favourite prayer is the prayer of the publican. It is like breathing, like the heartbeat of the world, the expression of its deepest longing for salvation and healing: 'Lord Jesus, be merciful to me a poor sinner!'

One desire still remains, that God would test him again in order to enable him, again and again and ever better, to find his depth in God, in order to be able with even more love to embrace that humble patience – the humility and patience that will make him like Jesus and enable God to perform his marvellous deeds in his life.

7

SPIRITUAL
COMPANIONSHIP

IN THE PREVIOUS chapter I spoke of the necessity of help or guidance in learning to attune ourselves to divine grace. In this chapter, therefore, I will say a word or two about the relationship between two people, one of whom attempts to give the other pointers on the quest for God and in living with God. The subject is spiritual guidance or, putting it in a way that sounds less directive and contains more respect for the person seeking guidance, spiritual companionship.*

The shift from the one expression to the other already indicates something of what may be considered one of the paradoxes of our time in the sphere of spiritual experience. On the one hand, immense resistance has arisen against concepts like 'spiritual father' or 'spiritual direction'. As a rule such terms are now carefully avoided, especially among persons who were formerly more or less obliged, for an extended period of time, to accept the status of being under the care of a spiritual father. Today there is often little mention of these concepts, and no one feels guilty. One can indeed appeal to modern achievements, the weight of which cannot be denied. Must not every believer be held personally accountable for his own spiritual adventure? Why should any person remain dependent on the judgement of another, someone who is at best a stranger and can only speak from the outside, and who at worst – a perennial risk – violates or paralyses one's own

---

*The original here, 'begeleiding', denotes the concept of accompaniment, familiar in English primarily from the sphere of music. To avoid this association I have opted for 'companionship'. *Translator.*

conscience instead of giving it space in which the freedom of the Holy Spirit can unfold?

But these days there is also the other side of the paradox. Seldom has the demand been so great and so urgent, among numerous young people and also among older persons, for some form of spiritual assistance. Many people, inside and outside the Church, who feel drawn toward some kind of spiritual adventure, go first in search of a guide, a mentor, a master. Today they confront the Church with their demand. And priests, religious, parents and lay people hear this demand coming from those who are searching for an answer, a Word, a *rhema* (as the ancient Fathers called it), in the strongest and most vital sense. But many of us, perhaps the majority, are unable to respond. Granted, we are acquainted with some good principles which we were once taught, and also with some fairly cheap recipes with which we ourselves have experimented more or less successfully. Certainly we can give people encouraging pats on the back in order, with the aid of some witticism, to elude the deeper issue, or we refer to the so-called 'harsh realities of life'. But actually we do not dare to give a genuine answer, not because we lack knowledge or book-learning, but simply because we do not have the personal experience. How can one speak of grace or of God when we have not personally had the experience of either?

These unanswered, or only half-answered, questions are undoubtedly one of the weakest areas in the life of the Church today. Consequently, some questioners have begun to knock on other doors, in churches of other denominations (even though their legacy in this field does not differ much from our own), or in non-Christian traditions from the East, where it was always obvious that internal experience could only be awakened or passed on by a Master.

The early monks of the fourth century had a saying attributed to St Anthony, recognized by everyone as the father of monks. It went like this, 'I know a number of monks,' said Anthony, 'who though they had practised much ascesis nevertheless fell. The reason was they had neglected the precept which says: "Ask your father and he will teach you." ' This saying appeals to the word of God itself (cf. Deut. 32:7) to justify spiritual guidance and shows that real spiritual experience without guidance runs serious risks.

Getting in touch with 'life'

What, after all, is at stake when a person seeks to deepen his, or her, spiritual life? He will begin to take seriously the seed of grace sown into him by baptism. Until then it was in fact but a seed. But to speak of a seed is to speak of the possibility of life. Stirring in every seed there is life. By nature the seed is called to develop, to germinate, to strike root – otherwise it is dead and useless. Life on the other hand is always in motion; it is active. Also, it develops in a certain direction. To take this life seriously is to take this development seriously, to remove barriers, to nourish it, and to let it come fully into its own.

For such is the nature of life. It would of course be easier if one could restrict faith to good catechetical instruction, to acquiring a few basic truths. Then it would be sufficient to commit these truths to memory in order, as time and occasion demanded, to draw the right conclusions.

Nor would it be any more difficult if faith were limited to a system of commandments and prohibitions. It would then be enough to allow one's attitude to be shaped by these. Similarly, if faith were primarily a project involving action or a way of winning, one could make oneself available. But faith, even though it demands to be expressed in a clear system of doctrine, is so much more than that. And even though it will bear fruit in a clear moral attitude and move the believer to involve himself effectively in the service of the kingdom of God on earth, this does not exhaust faith. Long before these things can happen, and at a level much more profound and basic than all this, faith is life, the life of God in us. It is life that must find its way through all the concrete realities of our human existence here on earth: the body, the heart, the soul, one's vocation, one's circumstances. It is life that can at the same time be promoted and hindered by all these things.

The believer's need then in the first place is not a catechist, a professor of morality, a vice-squad, or a specialist in grandly conceived pastoral projects. However necessary all these people may be, at this point we only need a person who from his or her own experience knows the interior life, who is also able to discern this life in others, to help them open their eyes to it and gradually to train them in cultivating it. In short, we need someone who can pass on to others the life of God that is in him or herself.

Now the ability to impart life is first of all a question of life itself. Nothing is more natural, nothing is less complicated for life than to propagate itself and strike root elsewhere. Life is of itself transparent, as it were, and comes across without difficulty. It propagates itself by osmosis. The ancient monks knew several versions of another saying, attributed to Abba Poimen, one of the most renowned of the Egyptian desert fathers. A monk asked him: 'Some brothers have come to live with me. Shall I lay down any rules for them?' 'Not at all,' answered the Abba. 'Do what you yourself have to do. If they really want to know the life, they must choose for themselves.' But the brother kept pressing for an answer: 'Abba, they want me to lay down something specific for them.' But Poimen replied: 'No way. Be a model for them, never a legislator.'

This feature of Christian monasticism reminds me of another saying, one that comes from the Hasidic tradition. A disciple tells how it was enough for him to watch his master as he (the master) was lacing his sandals. This small detail was enough to send him back deeply edified. A single gesture can be enough to pass on the message. For the real 'companions' are much more than teachers. They are themselves the teaching, their whole lives are the message. For life irresistibly awakens new life. And all the older person or guide needs to do is respond adeptly to the marvellous mystery of life. And they will do this best not by what they know, even less by what they may say, but simply by what they are able to pass on. What counts is the radiant quality of their being, that which they emit, often without knowing it, and without any need to express it in words.

By now it will be clear that spiritual companionship occurs at a certain level of what we call the human relationship. It is perhaps *the* relationship *par excellence*. After all, we are dealing with two people who come to be very close to each other and go for some distance on a journey together in the hope that between them something important may happen. It is as if a spark must leap from one to the other, the spark of life, not of any kind of life, but the life of God himself, something of the light and power of God's Spirit.

Of course this is primarily a spiritual happening. Still, this spiritual happening cannot for a moment be separated from the personal relationship which links the two people, and from the depth afforded them by way of this relationship. That depth serves the mystery of the Word of God that will again be enacted between the two, and this, as always, happens by becoming flesh and blood in the concreteness of their being. Hence the great importance of that human relationship and of its quality for spiritual companionship. It is without doubt the degree and quality of the shared experience that will trigger the event, and not the quantity – say, the number and duration of the conversations held or the length of the letters exchanged. On the contrary, quantity of contact may even be a hindrance and prevent things from happening if the two keep running fruitlessly around in their own little circle.

Spiritual companionship is one of the highest forms of human relationship. The Danish philosopher Kierkegaard calls the spiritual father 'more than a friend', and Dante, speaking of his guide Virgil, calls him 'more than a father'. The ancient Celtic concept of *amchara* means 'father of my soul', and Buddhist diction uses the word *lama*, 'incomparable mother'. Perhaps I may here refer also to the Greek Orthodox term by which a monk is denoted a *kaloiros*, that is 'a beautiful elder', a term which simultaneously suggests wisdom and warmth.

Like the Father

This leads to the question: What is that quality of being which awakens life in someone who has contact with it? Its name is *agape*, love. It is the comprehensive image of God, and of his Son when he lived among us; the spiritual companion will gradually become as an icon of the Son. On the face of a person, and through his or her conduct, something of the love of God will be manifest – that is, the tenderness and toughness that always marks the love of God. To see this is enough to turn us upside down, to change us from tip to toe. As a result, an unthought-of depth is revealed and comes to expression in us. In some cases, we even feel that at last we know who we are and why we exist. A new name is revealed to us, our real name. It is as if we are born again, this time to the only true life. The intense force of this reversal explains why, from the earliest generations of Christian believers, the words 'fatherhood' and 'motherhood' were used to express the relationship with the spiritual companion. This despite the warning of Jesus who seems to have expressly enjoined the opposite: 'Call no one on earth your father . . . or your master . . . one is your Father, one is your Master' (Matt. 23:9, 10). Yet, in several of his letters Paul already describes his activity as that of a father, or even a mother. He expressly claims to be a father, because he knows that by the gospel he fathered children in Christ Jesus (1 Cor 4:14–15). But he also thought of himself as a mother, for in another passage he describes how in his body he experienced the pangs of redemption till Christ was formed in his brothers (Gal. 4:19). Hence he is simultaneously father and mother, in the likeness of God, the Father of all fatherhood, and the Mother of all motherhood on earth.

Anyway, Jesus only asked his disciples not to claim the name 'father' for themselves. That request corresponds to one of the most fundamental conditions for the fruitfulness of spiritual companionship. No one should pose as father or have himself called father. No one should present himself as a guide to anyone. Usually the opposite occurs. It is not the father who chooses his pupil; it is the pupil who, as it were, recognizes his father – often after a long search. In a certain sense it may even be said that it is the role of the son to release the *charisma* of fatherhood in the father; it is the role of the pupil to give to the master an opportunity to disclose and validate himself. The inner disposition of the pupil is of great importance here. It is even necessary for the 'event' to occur. It is an attitude marked by availability, openness, watchfulness and patience, so as to awaken the slumbering presence of the guide or master in the other. A saying of the ancient fathers conveyed this idea in a rather abrupt way: 'Why is it that today's monks are no longer able to give a word of advice?' someone asked himself. And the answer was: 'Because the sons are no longer able to listen.' A Hindu saying states precisely the same truth: 'When the pupil is ready, the Master appears.'

The reason for this is that between master and pupil there exists a certain pre-existing mutual relationship, a reciprocally responsive attitude, a subtle rapport. While the key to our deeper being belongs to each of us personally, in most cases we are unable to find or use that key. Usually we need a word that comes to us from without, that strikes our inmost being and causes a hitherto unknown harmony to resonate in us. It is precisely this that the pupil unconsciously yearns for from the master. To be sure, he already carries it within himself; it is his deepest treasure and wealth. But left to himself he cannot fully reach it. He knows that his deepest secret can only be disclosed, in comprehension and love, by the other. Now it is this skill to bring out his inmost secret that the pupil unconsciously senses in the master he wants to have as his companion. At some point the master 'coincides' with his own depths, the better part of himself that he can only vaguely identify at this stage. That is also the reason why no one will be suited by just any guide. We are always better attuned to one specific person than to anyone else.

The thing that enables the 'companion' to surface for the pupil must in fact arise from the pupil's own heart. Accordingly, the words or gestures the master uses are of less importance; it is seldom their objective content that really matters. The words or external signs may equally well be only symbolic. The really important thing is the internal key of the pupil. We might also call it the interior master, *magister interior*, who is awakened in the heart of the pupil and from whom he will receive shape and life.

All this is even more important when that inner experience is a faith-experience and must therefore be in keeping with the dynamics peculiar to faith. The internal key, or the interior master we are dealing with here, is none other than the Holy Spirit himself. He is infallible and present in advance, long before we can perceive even the slightest spiritual desire in our heart. It is also he who will himself take our spiritual development in hand and guide it further in accordance with God's plan for us. Still, the intervention of the Holy Spirit does not make the presence of an outside companion superfluous. It is no less difficult, after all, to become sensitive to the activity of the Spirit in us and to interpret that activity in a correct and fruitful manner.

The intent of spiritual 'fatherhood' or 'motherhood' is to bring this new life, this new creation in the Holy Spirit, to birth. This occurs by thoughtfully accompanying the 'child' through the progressive transition from what the New Testament calls the 'old man' to the 'new man'. Contemporary psychology shows that on the psychological level something analogous has to occur. Maturity or maturation presupposes an ongoing transition from the superficial self to the deeper self and simultaneously an ongoing integration of the unconscious as it emerges into conscious daily life. In every human being there is hidden wealth, a treasure with which he has to be confronted, that he has to filter, order and absorb, that it may become useful in the exterior world. Thus life continues to grow, as a tree is able to bear new blossoms and fruit year after year. Thus over and over again, in every human being, a deeper reality is released, one that has to be integrated in that person's conduct, including his love relationships. This is a sign that life is still actively present in a person, that it has not yet become paralysed or set, and is still able to bear new fruit.

The same thing is true of regeneration by the Holy Spirit or, as Paul put it, the continued growth toward the full measure of the mature person in Jesus Christ (Eph. 4:13). This emergence of 'the new man' is essentially interwoven with each person's psychology. The companion will always have to bear this in mind. He or she will never be able to make a clear distinction in the psyche between a purely psychological reality and what could come only from the Holy Spirit. In the event of a surgical intervention a surgeon can clearly distinguish between a nerve, a muscle, or a blood vessel, but in one's internal experience this sort of distinction is not possible. Everything is essentially psychological, and at the same time either in harmony with the Spirit or not. That means that the Spirit's activity can press equally against the dark sides as against the light sides of the personality. Psychological balance is not a condition for spiritual progress, and psychic weakness is never an insuperable obstacle. Everything depends on discerning how the dark sides and the light sides are employed, and in what direction the two develop, to the advantage or disadvantage of the inner person and, finally, of love.

This is the main concern of spiritual companionship or 'fatherhood'. It will attempt to accompany and to clarify this process. We could say, in other words, that it comes down to the discovery of what is currently called the 'interiority' that is present in every human being. It is our inmost being, our most interior reality, our deepest level. To let this inmost being come to the surface, and to awaken a new sensitivity to spiritual values, is something we cannot manage on our own. A person has to be somehow started on the way. We need a little help in order to come to terms with this newness, and to discover and recognize our best self in the process. In that sense spiritual companionship has to do with what, since Socrates, has been called *maieutics*, midwifery, and the companion is somewhat like the midwife or nurse.

This may be the reason why Thomas Merton in one of his last books, *Final Integration: Toward a Monastic Therapy*, ventures to speak of an attempt to be 'fully born', to come fully into the world. By this he means someone who is able to live from within his inner experience which he can discern and can feel welling up in the depths of his interior being. When this integration succeeds, it is a source of great maturity and of more than common wisdom. For the deep ground of a human being is much more universal than the empirical, superficial ego. The person who has got in touch with this ground of his or her being has become a cosmic person, the universal human-being. He has attained a more complete identity than that of his tiny, limited ego which is a mere fragment of his true being. He can now also identify with all other human beings and immerse himself in their lives. He has become a universal, world-wide person, a fountain of love for all. For he can enter everyone's love and pain and still remain free toward all. He has touched the source of freedom in the ground of his being. This is the freedom of the Holy Spirit. He is no longer led mainly by his will, by noble examples or noble feelings, nor by his rational intellect. Now he can begin to live spontaneously from within, from the source of his being that is God himself. True spontaneity is the sign of inner freedom. It is spontaneous, unconstrained action proceeding from love, in accord with his inmost being. This is perhaps the sense in which Augustine's dictum *Ama et fac quod vis* (Love, and do what you want) must be understood. For it is enough to love, or to love still more.

Here we can easily answer a question that is often asked: is spiritual companionship absolutely necessary for a deep life of faith? The possibility that God should intervene directly to guide someone is never excluded. This is not, however, his usual way of acting. Someone who would reach a deep level of intense spiritual life normally depends on help from a certain kind of companionship. This is true not only during the early stages, when it is easy to accept that initiation by another is necessary. It applies also later, especially at moments when a person is called by the Holy Spirit to take an important step forward. Each time it is as if he or she has to cross an unfamiliar threshold in order to live on a, till this moment, strange and totally new level. These are always times of uncertainty, when a person does not know what direction to take. Illusions threaten on every side and questions pile up. One must pass through a labyrinth of numerous and often subtle reactions of self-love and injured pride, must attempt to recover the fine thread of grace, and must try to maintain and trace the gentle and almost unsearchable urging of the Holy Spirit. It is this urging to which we must always remain open, and which will some day seize us in order to separate us from ourselves and to lead us on further to a place where we would perhaps not have wanted to go if left to ourselves – to something which no eye has seen, nor ear heard, and which has never occurred in the human heart.

The fact that at some point we may feel again the need for spiritual guidance is only a sign that such a decisive moment has dawned. We again have dire need for a guide. But then we may also be sure, with a certainty drawn from faith, that that guide stands ready for us. If we only look longingly for such a guide, God will put him on our way. Do not look for the guide too far away and do not aim too high, for even the last and the least of one's brothers or sisters may surprise you with a word that is indeed a Word of God – the condition being that you were genuinely waiting for it.

Uncovering one's desires

We have just seen how the quality of spiritual companionship depends mainly on the quality of the inter-human relationship. Now the quality of that relationship depends largely on the quality of the conversation that takes place between the two partners in the relationship. The whole tradition of spiritual direction is agreed on this: companionship is especially a matter of conversation and dialogue; the pupil comes to interrogate his 'father' and expects from him a word he can live by. The aim of the conversation is also fairly clear – the disclosure of one's thoughts. But what does this mean?

First of all, it must be plain to the reader that we make a distinction between spiritual companionship and the sacrament of reconciliation. In confession one confesses to a priest, who is the administrator of the sacrament, the sins which one has committed and for which one begs forgiveness. That confession may be the starting-point of a good spiritual conversation that may eventually follow. But in itself this is not necessary. When absolution has been given, confession is complete and in a sense is finished.

On the other hand, a pastoral conversation is not necessarily linked with confession. In most cases it is not. Accordingly, the spiritual companion does not have to be a priest. Spiritual assistance has nothing to do with priesthood. A layperson, man or woman, who has had personal experience of life in the Holy Spirit, can render this assistance as well as a priest who has had little or no such experience. In any case, one does not primarily tell the spiritual companion of the sins one has committed but rather of what the ancient texts call 'thoughts' or *logismoi*. By this they did not mean so much what we *think* but rather what we *sense*, what we *strive after*: feelings, yearnings and inclinations that freely arise in one's heart and imagination, even though they seldom or never become full-fledged sins.

Accordingly, the word 'confess' would be inappropriate here. The only thing we are dealing with is *'disclosure'*, bringing to light, in the presence of one's partner in conversation. The person unburdening himself is not asking for forgiveness, not even for encouragement – and certainly not for reassurance, however it may appear; but more on this later. What he expects in the first place is *acceptance.* The fact that he may express in the other person's presence the longings and feelings that have for so long been suppressed and bottled up in his inmost being is already for him an extraordinary happening, and already brings enormous relief. He is no longer alone with his burden. He can and may pass it to another, someone who quietly looks at it and accepts it in love. After all, such acceptance has everything to do with love.

Accordingly, the first moments of the spiritual conversation, when these most questionable feelings at last rise to the surface, are the most important. At this point the honesty and genuineness of the love of the companion – here, I dare say, of the father – will be tested. Some companions make the mistake of opening their mouth too quickly, whether to disapprove or to condone. The reason why this is a serious error will be explained in the following section. What needs to be briefly emphasized here is that an attentive and loving ear and the absorption of what is being confided is of decisive importance for the future of the relationship. Again, the purpose is not to approve or disapprove of the inclinations and desires of the person, but to accept that person as he has presented himself, burdened with the feelings he has only with much difficulty been able to express. That person has the right to be as he is, as he feels, and as he has laid himself open – together with all the desires or longings he has revealed. For the time being one must not ask whether they are good or bad. This is true even when they are expressed in what on first hearing sounds just like gibberish.

Still, and here we face the most delicate challenge for spiritual companionship, somewhere in this gibberish, which as such is and remains unacceptable, occurs the hard-to-decipher articulation of deep but still unfulfilled human desires that are not only fundamental but also perfectly healthy. The fact that those desires are enmeshed in gibberish is merely a relative evil. As a rule it has more to do with clumsiness, inexperience, mishaps in the past and the distortions that followed and are not the responsibility of the victim, than with real sin. Through his gibberish this basic healthiness must be recognized and affirmed, and also, to the degree this is possible, its profound genuineness respected in a creative way. This is also the only way in which we can ever connect with God's mercy and with the grace that comes to affirm every person as a human being down to his deepest human weakness and to reinstate him.

This undoubtedly lies behind the familiar advice St Benedict passes on to the abbot: *Oderit vitia, diligat fratres*; He shall hate the defects but love the brothers (*Rule*, ch. 64:11). The brother must feel loved by the abbot as he is, despite his weakness, indeed including his weakness. He is worthy of love as he is, without conditions. There are no conditions of eligibility for being loved; no mistakes which disqualify one from receiving love. This is true for us as it is for God. Here the spiritual father is at his best; he becomes an icon of the heavenly Father, who makes his sun to rise on the good and on the evil (Matt. 5:45); an icon also of Jesus who came to call not the righteous but sinners (Mark 2:17).

The fact that long-suppressed feelings and desires rise to the surface in spiritual conversation is important not only because then they can at last be valued at their true worth and perhaps even honoured; its importance lies primarily in the fact that we can now delve more deeply into ourselves. For this is necessary if grace is to come fully into its own in our lives. Our greatest needs, after all, are not of an intellectual or ideological kind. Nor do they lie at the level of our willpower or capacity for active involvement. Grace digs down more deeply into a person. It connects with our deepest, most inexpressible desires, the place where we feel most injured and indescribably weak. It is the place where, according to Paul, desires of the Spirit are opposed to the flesh and the desires of the flesh are opposed to the Spirit (Gal. 5:17). 'Flesh', in the Pauline sense, must be taken here to mean our deep human desires. *There* lies the point of contact between God's grace and our self, the meeting-place where Spirit and flesh vie against each other and fight each other with opposing desires. But it is also the place where we can be sure we can get into touch with grace. For us to be able to hear the desires of the Spirit in ourselves, the desires of the flesh must first rise to the surface and be discernible. How could the Spirit, who constantly contends with the flesh, be discerned where the flesh is not clearly discernible? It is therefore of greatest importance that we can be confronted with our own deepest desires, that we can quietly observe them without fear and without rashness, in order that the deep insistence of the Spirit can also rise to the surface in us. Here the purpose of spiritual companionship is to bring us closer to our deepest feelings in order to bring us closer to the Holy Spirit.

Internal censorship

We saw above how it is the task of the companion to awaken in his pupil the internal master, in our case the Holy Spirit. Before he can do this he will inevitably come into conflict with the one who, in each of us, is the adversary and sworn enemy of our internal master, and whom I shall call here the internal 'censor' or 'police officer'. One of the first tasks of the companion is to discern in the conversation the presence of that internal police officer.

The reader who knows something of psychology will already understand what is meant by the expression 'the internal police officer'. It is the superego, which we now know to be a necessary part of every human psyche. In our moral conduct it plays a predominant role which no one can escape and of which the actual results can be either paralysing or liberating. In any case, the superego must be won over and restored by grace. It is in each of us an unconscious agency that exercises an authority over the practical options open to us. It is the crystallization of all the imprints our experience of authority has left in each of us. We still today hear in it the echoes, disapproving or encouraging, of orders, commands and prohibitions we received in the past, of punishment we were subjected to, of threats and guilt imposed on us. Needless to say, the parental figure, or rather the imprints which our parents rightly or wrongly made on us, play a decisive role in the formation of the superego. But other authority figures – like teachers, youth leaders or priests – have also, for good or ill, left their tracks behind in us. Just as in childhood I was controlled more or less strictly by my parents, so I am today still assisted or pursued by the equally severe and demanding interventions of the internal agency I call here the internal police officer. He is the bogeyman who stops me, who stands in my way, and often causes me to fail. He threatens and intimidates me; he even punishes me and pushes me around, generating feelings of guilt and shame.

The difficulty most of us experience in laying bare our feelings and desires to another person derives not so much from the fact that they are actually wrong but primarily from the unconscious judgement the internal police officer pronounces over them.

When we feel timid or ashamed in front of our spiritual companion, this arises from the fact that we project upon him or her the value judgements we are incurring all the time from our internal censor. In this unconscious identification by the pupil of his internal policeman with his spiritual companion lies the possibility of a genuine liberation but also the risk that master and pupil may get hopelessly stuck in it. This happens when the spiritual companion unconsciously assumes the place of the internal police officer and, even with the best of intentions, only heightens and reinforces the negative influence of the latter.

This happens much more quickly and more often than we think, and in most cases long before we are aware of it. For that matter, when in the conversations the pupil does not manage to express his deepest feelings freely there is little chance of anything else happening. The classic mode of spiritual companionship, as followed up to recently, was certainly not devoid of results. It ran the danger, however, of setting itself on the side of the internal censor. With some slight exaggeration we could describe it as follows. The spiritual father was especially concerned to instil solid convictions in his spiritual son. Accordingly, he fed him a diet of ideals; youth, after all, had to dream of ideals and devote their energies to them. The patient's will-power was firmly whipped up. When burdened or defeated he was given encouragement. When he had erred in some fashion, use was made of the well known threats normally associated with mortal sin. To bring about amendment of life, at best a concrete plan of mortification was sketched out in which a strategy of hard and difficult training (to guard against yielding to the next temptation) played an undeniably central role – all this naturally with the help of the grace of God – something that was assumed but hardly came into its own in the strategy planned.

The weak point of this type of spiritual companionship lies precisely in the fact that the companion relates only to the superego, to the person's internal police officer. There is a great danger then that he will never connect with the internal master, or with the grace of the Holy Spirit, the source of real freedom. The companion will not only fail to act liberatingly and to generate life, but the effect of his efforts will be as anxiety-producing as the internal censure itself. This will be the case even if he makes much of the word 'freedom'. For there is a way of handling the concept of freedom that only turns it into an extra obligation and so unconsciously adds to the person's confusion.

Taking the place of the internal police officer can occur very easily. One cannot be too careful. It would happen the moment the companion says something like: 'It is again your own fault'; 'You should be ashamed of yourself'; 'You are unpardonably weak'. But it can happen just as much, and be equally pernicious, when the companion offers enthusiastic approval or firmly attempts to oppose guilt feelings: 'Bravo, that was really good!'; 'There is no harm in that'; 'Nowadays that is all OK'. All these pronouncements fit in well with the voice of the superego. If the companion permits himself to take this second, tempting line, he again falls into the same role. He fails to distance himself from the level of focusing only on 'what is allowed' and 'what is not allowed', 'what is permitted' and 'what is forbidden'. He still takes the place of the police officer.

A very acute, and therefore transparent, case is that of the person with extreme scruples. Such a person is totally subject to his or her internal censor and is no longer able even to choose between good and evil. He can only carry out in fear and trembling what that internal agency has imposed on him as an obligation, even when it flies in the face of all common sense, something of which he himself is often clearly aware. To help him one could try to ease his scruples by making encouraging statements like: 'But that is not wrong'; 'You really did not intend to do that'; 'Actually you were not free at the time'. But experience teaches that the relief thus offered is of short duration. Nor is this surprising. By using this language one again assumes the place of the internal police officer. Where he usually condemns, you now acquit. The result of this acquittal is however short-lived. The moment you are gone the old anxiety returns, for the internal tyrant resumes his job and everything starts again from scratch.

The question is how to help a person under the sway of the internal policeman, even if his problems are not as acute as those of the over-scrupulous person. The first condition concerns the affective quality of the relationship; it needs a strong dose of genuine love. From the person being helped love emerges as profound trust; in the companion it shows itself in openness and the capacity to listen and absorb. Only under these conditions can the new affective bond between companion and pupil gradually offset the affective bond which ties the latter to his superego. For the tie between him and his superego, however interwoven with guilt and anxiety, is also powerfully charged emotionally. That which was commanded or forbidden us by parents or some other authority always had to do with the love we might receive from them. Behind every feeling of dread instilled in us by the internal police officer sounds an echo of what we heard earlier in life, even if it was only implied: 'If you do not do such or such, you will lose my love.' For that reason the love that is conveyed in the actual relationship between companion and pupil is *very* important. For only genuine love will ultimately be able to counter the power of the internal censor.

The second condition is that from his position of love the companion is able at the appropriate time to deal with the pupil's internal censor. He can, of course, be sure that the other's censor will attack him as well. Initially the censor will try to get the companion on his side. As we saw above, the companion will have to be very careful not to fall into the role of censor and he will therefore avoid anything that might prompt this. He will be careful to avoid taking over the censor's language and vocabulary (like 'You should really . . .', or 'What you ought to do in fact . . .'). In that way he will

neither induce fear or guilt, nor be excessively indulgent and
exonerating, and there is then a chance that the internal
censor will lose his hold on the victim. The censor's power is
reduced; he is striking out in a vacuum.

In time there will come a moment when the companion
can, within the heart of the relationship as it were, deal the
death-blow to the internal police officer of the other and
eliminate him. How this is to be done is hard to describe, but
the truth is that it does happen. And it happens simply in the
course of *living*. It springs unexpectedly from the companion,
as a spark of life and freedom that leaps over to the other. It
derives from the life and the beginning of real freedom that
already pervades the companion. He is suddenly allowed to
checkmate the other's internal censor, to touch the other at a
much deeper level of his person, the place where life lies
hidden behind all the shame and *angst*. The art is to liberate
this life by love and to reinforce that which lies concealed deep
within the scruples. And I may add, deep in what appears at
first sight to be evil. For absolute evil is rare among humans;
in most cases it is merely a distorted good. The spiritual father
then knows how, by love, to straighten out the distortion. For
the moment the distortion has been undone the evil is gone
and genuine life can freely well up afresh. Then it also
becomes clear that sin is not where we have usually feared it
to be, and that the good is not always to be found where we
have usually sought it. Good and evil are somewhere else.
They exist not simply on the surface, but at a much deeper
level – close to where God is in us. And without God's light
and God's look at us we are totally unable to say anything
about it. All this applies to ourselves, and even more in the
case of others. 'Do not judge, that you be not judged' (Matt.
7:1).

What we have just described does not happen all at once,
in a single conversation; it is a life process. Nor is the spiritual
companion the main actor. He makes himself available to the
work of a divine power within himself. That deathblow to the
distorting power in the other is ultimately a product of
the Word of God, of his Spirit and his overwhelming love.
The event of being taken up, with all one's sin and weakness,
into the love of a spiritual father is the sign – we daresay 'the

sacrament' – of being taken up into the mercy of God. There
is love and inexpressible joy. Here we again encounter real
penthos, evangelical grief and remorse. Nothing is so liberating,
so deeply affirming, as genuine repentance. That repentance,
however, has nothing to do with the guilt feelings triggered
in us by the internal censor. He is also undoubtedly the one
who attempts to block genuine repentance. Psychological guilt
feeling and an evangelical sense of sin are two different things.
In the case of genuine repentance one knows oneself to be
taken up in love and gratitude together with all one's sins and
weaknesses. For it is only in our weakness that the power of
God comes into its own.

Once the internal police officer has been removed the companion effortlessly assumes leadership. I mean the real companion, the Holy Spirit, before whom the human companion
may withdraw himself. This occurs as soon as the pupil himself is in touch with the Spirit and has learned, based on
this connection, to live freely and spontaneously. Here the
genuinely Christian conscience is born: 'For all who are led
by the Spirit of God are children of God' (Rom. 8:14 NRSV).

The mirror image

Besides the internal censor we carry in our psyches still
another agency that may hinder our connection with the grace
of God, and spiritual companionship may also help with this.
I mean the ideal self, the mirror-image of myself which in the
course of time I have constructed for myself and to which I
am as passionately attached and enslaved as I am (or was)
to my internal censor.

Everyone knows the myth of Narcissus who fell in love with
his reflection in the pool and drowned when he reached out
to embrace it. This myth expresses part of our humanity in
a symbolic way. Our ideal self-image is always more beautiful
than we are in reality. It is a highly charged human and also
spiritual ideal. Everything I do or fail to do, everything I
achieve or fail to achieve, is unconsciously measured against
the standard of this ideal self-image. I would love to be the
person I am not and refuse to be the person I in fact am. My
ideal self-image is the cheap consolation by means of which

I try, in an acceptable way, to make my way in life. Even if I should fail and come to grief, I can still console myself by casting a sideways glance at my ideal self-image toward which I know I am moving.

In the context of spiritual companionship this mirror image of the self is another delicate issue. It again involves a serious risk. The mirror image may be reinforced by a naive companion, who may take it over from the pupil and unconsciously act from that angle – applauding when the pupil lives up to something in the mirror image and disapproving when he fails. The fact that he has taken over this mirror image is not primarily his fault. From the start the pupil unconsciously brought this about. For lack of a truer self-image the pupil presented himself to his companion under the likeness of the unconscious ideal he had constructed for himself. And because nothing was more reassuring to the two partners, the companion eagerly adopted it. From then on he also serves the mirror image; the other simply annexed him for his own purpose.

Now the way God teaches us is precisely opposite to this. God employs every means to shatter the mirror and the image. When at last this occurs, it may have shocking consequences. As a result of such an experience the apostle Paul fell from his horse, struck to the ground, and was blind for three days. In order to become an apostle he could not continue to live by the mirror image of Jewish legalistic perfection; on the contrary, he had to be reconciled with his weakness and limitations, eventually with his spiritual dividedness and sinfulness. Before he encountered Jesus this could not have happened, but it did happen the very moment Jesus appeared to him.

As is evident from this incident in Paul's life and from numerous other conversion stories, the sudden loss of the mirror-image is an extremely shocking event to someone who has lived by it for years. He seems to have lost his footing, is shaken to his foundations. And indeed, the ground has been moved from under his feet, the ground on which until then he had built his personality. It is one of those moments on the spiritual path when a person may be on the verge of a psychic collapse. It is a danger that will only be averted by

what is revealed to him at such a time of the love and boundless mercy of God – that is, of grace. In the light of such an
experience Paul could later say with strong conviction: 'By
the grace of God I am what I am' (1 Cor. 15:10).

At such a crucial moment the only task of the companion
is to promote that saving encounter with God or at least keep
the road open for it. For not until the mirror of his ideal self-
image has been smashed is the road at last open. Accordingly,
he will above all resist the temptation to gather up the fragments of the mirror-image with the intention of restoring it
in its original form. Nothing could be more damaging, even
though at first the pupil would feel considerably relieved by
this. However, no new mirror-image may be constructed,
under any pretext! On the contrary, the pupil must learn to
accept the broken pieces of the first image, without bitterness,
quietly and resignedly, and soon afterwards with gratitude
and hope in his heart. In most cases he will be able to do this
only with the calm acceptingness and loving understanding
he experiences from his companion during this time of crisis.

For the companion will often be the first sign and channel
by which the love of God is made plain to his shattered pupil.
After all, only when the mirror and his ideal self-image have
been shattered does the road lie open before him. This is of
absolute importance. For the inmost secret of a human being
does not lie locked up in the mirror-image he has formed of
himself. It lies much deeper in him, and can be disclosed
only by another, and that in love. Then the first person he
encounters is usually the spiritual father. Much will then
depend on this contact and on the fact that he can read his
deepest self in the other's words and responses, whether or
not it is reflected in his eyes and his love. The idea is not that
he should immerse and lose himself in the companion but
that he should be gathered up, understood, and confirmed by
the other in his best self, in his most profound and authentic
identity.

This then is the moment in which a word, a real *word*,
becomes possible and is even urgently expected. But not until
this point. We pointed out earlier that in the initial stages of
the conversation the companion has to be very careful in the
use of words. Too often the words used are premature and

can actually damage the dialogue or even cut it short. However, when a climate of trust and love has been established, when anxiety and shame have been totally separated from all the feelings and longings that were expressed with so much difficulty, then comes the hour in which a word, however slight, can bear considerable fruit. Then a single word, spoken in love and with the proper emphasis, is often amply sufficient. In the mouth of the companion a word then regains the primitive power it should always possess. It is again creative and life-giving, like the Word of God. It possesses the power to regenerate a human being.

Such a word strikes at a very deep level in us. It touches the source of our freedom which is also the source of our capacity to love. It stirs up and releases us to freedom. And, in the light of that newly won freedom, all other things can be properly evaluated.

At this point there is also the possibility of intuiting where sin has been hiding. Something that was strongly felt to be evil proves in retrospect to have been innocent; something that passed for virtue and righteousness is revealed as being ridden and interwoven with sin. Often a great deal of hidden pride comes unexpectedly to light but especially lack of love and childlike trust in God. Someone able to correctly intuit the presence of sin in himself is also immediately ready to be engulfed by the divine mercy and find his deepest joy in tears of repentance. Here they are again! Nothing is more liberating. Not for nothing have many authors, beginning with the most ancient, repeated over and over in the course of ages that we must be born again out of the tears of repentance and that only in such tears would the waters of baptism bear their most abundant fruit.

The true God for the free person

According to Benedict the spiritual father must carefully watch to see if the novice 'truly seeks God' (*si vere Deum quaerit, Rule* 58.7). One could also construe this clause differently: 'if he seeks the *true* God'. The question is whether he may be pursuing a false God whose image he is carrying in his inmost being. We must find the true God who will make us free in the encounter with him. The spiritual father must himself come to recognize this God, and have a feeling for real freedom. Freedom is the reflection of God in a human being. This is what the spiritual father must be able to assess in the other. He must be able to tell what is going on in the other: at what point the other is fettered in slavery; at what point he threatens to close up despite his external piety or virtue. He must take particular note of the internal censor that is at work and of the authority and influence exerted by the person's own mirror-image. This requires discernment, *diakrisis*. the ability to distinguish spirits. The true God is not the God of a person's convictions or of his noble-mindedness but, as Ruysbroek strikingly put it, the God who 'comes at us from the inside to the outside', the God of whom one becomes aware from within.

Because it is so important to discern the symptoms of unfreedom in others, I want to spend a few moments here describing some of them. It is not hard, because in the case of the unfree person only part of him comes into its own; the rest has disappeared from the foreground. This type of person is frequently encountered these days. In these people social qualities are foremost – intellect, will-power, generosity – qualities which are often mistakenly interpreted as signs of faith and superhuman conduct. Kept in the background – often silenced, suppressed, or at least strongly censured – are the vital forces which should convey life. As a rule these forces are considered suspect and are distrusted; suspicions about them are never fully expressed but nevertheless they carry a lot of power. Some of these vital forces are tenderness and love (often confused with sensuality and selfishness); resoluteness and forcefulness (often confused with lovelessness and a lack of attention to others); a capacity for vigorous and thorough action (confused with hardness); a feeling for beauty (confused with superfluous luxury); self-confidence (confused with pride).

All these are deep human qualities that should be made available to the kingdom of God. They are not only basic human qualities that should be honoured in a person but are also indispensable to the kingdom of God. They must therefore not be kept under lock and key but be made available for purification. Usually, however, they are kept back and not taken at their true value with a view to their being taken up into the dynamics of the Holy Spirit who in his love and power enlarges and develops them.

These are a few of the features which characterize the inwardly divided persons we often encounter. This inner dividedness is a heavy burden for the person concerned. An enormous amount of energy is lost in such a person. He is unconsciously forced to invest a vast amount of energy in keeping all these things in the background. In those people in whom the ego and psychic structure are weak this is even dangerous. But in most people a viable compromise is found. Such a person may then go on living a peaceful life, but does so with a dulled mind. Shutting himself off from love, he locks himself into an assortment of roles that, while they absorb all his energies, secure him against the demands and risks of genuine love.

It would not be hard to list even more such symptoms which suggest that a person is not yet in touch with his deeper self, nor acting out of his deepest life-source. Examples are certain forms of fanaticism: being far to the political left or to the right, extremely progressive or conservative, very spiritual or very secular. Actually, these are merely other names for the idealized mirror-image of a person or for the tyranny exercised by the superego. Illness and chronic fatigue may also indicate that a person is subject to too much stress, as do the tasks one creates for oneself unasked, or has been assigned but carries out in a typically frenetic manner. In all monasteries one encounters monks who are busier than the pope. Some forms of activism – the inability to say no, to quit working, to take a break, to go to bed on time – are symptoms of inner tension. So too are forms of ritualism in which some people lock themselves up and waste much time.

One's colleagues and friends usually have a sharp eye for such symptoms. In popular parlance one hears telling things on this point. For example: 'Take that task away from him and you will kill him.' Or with regard to someone who is ill: 'If he should get better he will die of the consequences.' Or: 'If the doctor were to take his medicine away from him, he would be sure to get sick.' About someone excessively virtuous they say in French: 'Il est un dragon de vertu!' ('He is a dragon of virtue!'). Of someone who imposes a heavy work schedule on himself and others it is said: 'He is a workaholic'; or of someone who is submerged by his work: 'He works himself to death'. One may well ask who here is the victim and who the executioner. If it is said about a meticulously observant monk that he is a 'living rule', that is certainly deserving of respect, providing that besides that 'living rule' something else is also alive in the man; perhaps people mean that the rest of the man is dead. Outwardly, to a degree and for a time, such a lifestyle can be satisfactory, one may even occasionally be applauded. But in fact all this has a crippling effect. Such people never develop into full maturity. They are not really content or happy, because they remain turned in upon themselves. In their relations with others they are not really open or capable of acting freely on their own. They may be the heroes of their duty – or, who knows, victims of their duty – but they do not pass on life. They are sterile and barely manage to stay alive. They need all their energy to keep the process going. Only death will liberate them – unless they risk being confronted with their weakness in the presence, and with the help, of a spiritual father!

Key aspects of companionship

Earlier we saw that at certain times spiritual companionship is usually indispensable. Here I wish to comment on three situations: discerning the will of God, awakening our inner self, and surrendering to God's activity in us.

First, then, the issue of *discerning the will of God*. This may entail a fundamental choice, a call, for example, or a vocation, or the choice of a life-companion. But it may also entail one of the many minor choices continually forced upon us in our daily life, choices that frequently pull us in opposite directions. Still, we want to make a good choice; that is, we want to make a choice in accordance with God's purpose for us. I am referring here to the sort of situation in which many people would in any case turn to another person for advice.

When we come to our companion with this question, it is

not because we think that person has a ready-made answer, either from personal wisdom or insight, or because he has received a special illumination from God to pass on to us. On the contrary, the spiritual father has no solution at hand. He himself knows this all too well. The answer lies with us – in our own heart. It was given us in advance, in the inmost part of our being, by the Spirit of God given to us. This means that what we are looking for as the will of God for us is already somewhere in our possession, and that it cannot therefore be so very difficult to discover. From experience we know that in previous instances it was difficult to arrive at a responsible decision – just as we are aware that in the past, in similar circumstances, we erred from time to time. Maybe we were convinced that a certain course of action was the will of God, but in retrospect we saw it to have been a painful illusion which kept alive in us some hard-to-discern and even harder-to-express bent or inclination, though we were totally unaware of this at the time.

This should not really surprise us, if we call to mind that the will of God is always in some mysterious way involved in the complex tangle of desires and fears we mentioned earlier. This tangle of hard-to-unravel desires is far from being our deepest self. It is located on the surface of our being like a wall or a kind of cloak through which it is not easy to discern the will of God. And it is made all the harder by the fact that God's desires are interwoven with our own. Could it be otherwise?

The task of the spiritual father, however, is not to break down the wall, or to lift the cloak. Actually, this is not something he is able to do. And even if someone could do it, the result would at first be such a shock and so confusing that it would be better to spare anyone such a trial. The first thing the spiritual father will do here is again to take everything in. Through and behind all the trivial little whims and desires that tear our hearts and that we can disclose only with difficulty and sometimes with shame, a sensitive ear, and a heart that is pure, will be able to detect the desire for God which is hidden deep in our heart, the will of God which lies at the source and origin of our being. When the companion thinks he has tracked it down, it is still not for him to impose on us this purpose of God; that could not lead to any satisfactory result. But he could help us to come to a place where we would be able to pick ourselves up and disentangle our desires, for example by posing a number of objective questions, in the most neutral tone possible, and especially by throwing light on our desires from the Bible.

In that way we will gradually come to see where the difference lies between our little desires and the will of God. For as soon as we are genuinely able to see through our own little desires and become conscious of where and how they constantly threaten to crowd out the will of God, a spontaneous desire arises in us to give up these whims and to freely yield ourselves to the will of God. For the will of God is not only the desire for God, it is also the power of God, power that is always available to us. The moment we are enabled to discern clearly what the will of God for us is, it surges in on us with a clarity that overwhelms us, but without doing violence. It will gently take our free will in tow, so that it can only yield itself up, the way one joyfully surrenders oneself to love. This is real freedom. How could the will of God not succeed with us? It forms a part of the deep core of our being. It is what we already are; it will also guide us toward our full personal maturity. Someone who has had a different experience with and differing memories of the will of God thereby shows that it has not yet been given to him really to discern God within himself.

A second important aspect of spiritual experience is the *awakening of our inner self.* Usually this happens in prayer, a subject to which we will return later. For the moment it is enough for us to furnish some pointers on the role of the spiritual companion in this connection. For it is an important moment when prayer has to flow, as it were, from outside our being to inside. In some of us this is already happening at the beginning of our spiritual life. In most, however, it happens only after many years. By that time prayer has long ceased to be unfamiliar. We can boast of some practice and experience. We have journeyed on a number of prayer routes and tried out several prayer methods.

Nor was it always fruitless. Some technique or other seemed

to suit us, at least for a while. In time we may become familiar with a prayer routine that does not altogether displease us: a bit of Bible reading every day, a few moments of what we call reflection or meditation, a few prayer formulas or ejaculatory prayers. We are inclined to be content with this routine and not to demand more than seems reasonable, and this is already a great deal more than most committed and involved believers are still willing to achieve.

There comes a moment, however, at which God can no longer be satisfied with this. To persuade us to look beyond this prayer routine and to embark on the open seas he has a very effective means at his disposal; he cuts off the current and turns off the tap. At that very moment everything stops and everything dries up – intellect, imagination, feelings – all the capacities which from time to time we employed so busily as we prayed – now begin to wrestle with an insurmountable feeling of boredom, sometimes to the point of despair. Does this mean that our attempts to pray are irrevocably doomed to fail? On the contrary, it is precisely the opposite that is now made available to us, and by God himself. The only real chance of prayer now stands before our door, if only we dare to open that door and let it in. For it is God who is taking the situation in hand; it is he who wants to shift to a higher gear and expects us to do the same. However, this never occurs without an initial time of perplexity and sometimes even of confusion.

Now at least we are on the threshold of the mystery that, once we have taken this step, will never release us from its spell. What step? The question is wrongly put. We do not even need to take a step. How could we – in our own strength? It is enough to drop a number of things, that is, to open our hands and let go of all the unnecessary things that have accumulated in our heart and block any movement at a deeper level in ourselves. It is not about doing more; on the contrary; it is about doing much less. We need to release our grip on many things and events, also our grip on prayer, and in a way to fall over backwards, to tumble down into our inner self, toward this still unfamiliar world of our deepest depths, to this best side of ourselves that at some point mysteriously connects with God and flows into him. There opens a dizzying abyss of which, over a long part of our life, we were unaware, but which simultaneously attracts us and fills us with dread the moment we have some inkling of it.

At this juncture we usually again need the help of a companion, not to give us a little push in a direction we have not yet decided to take, but to help us become conscious of that awed sense of inner dizziness that calls us to surrender to it. It is God in his own person in the deepest depths of our heart who constitutes this dizziness. He is the source of prayer in us, a source that has only to be opened up. Blessed is the heart in which that source has been unstopped and can well up freely, thanks to a single word, a single glance sometimes, from a colleague or a friend who came to stand beside us.

A third important aspect of every spiritual experience is getting to know the way in which God is at work within us and how we may connect with him. In a word, it is the acquisition of a *new* way – the only real way *of co-operating with God, by surrendering to God's activity in us.* Just as we always have a tendency to go our own way in prayer, so we also run the risk of wanting to map out the conditions for an active and fully engaged faith-life in the service of God's kingdom. It is as if it were not God who builds his kingdom and we who are merely his servants, nor that the only important thing is that here too we trace God's activity in us which will little by little take over our activity.

This presupposes a profound transformation in our usual way of doing things. God would love to teach us how we can effectively open ourselves up and yield to the power that is his and that is constantly, like a hurricane, breaking out over the world and the Church. However, we have little capacity to observe that power of God as long as we are on the wrong wavelength; or, if we have somehow managed to find the right wavelength, we easily block God's activity by our own 'broadcasts' and over-hasty initiatives, however well intended. It would be good if once in a while we took time to pause and listen in silence so that God's activity has a chance to rise to the surface of our heart. The moment we become aware of the signs of this activity – and as a rule the signs leave no room for doubt – it is enough for us to surrender totally to it.

In short, the idea is to learn to take leave of a well-intentioned but often ill-considered activism, and to switch over in the action itself to a certain passivity which gives God the best chance to unfold his activity in us to the fullest possible extent. This change is not always obviously to our advantage. It involves, pain. It is a paschal cup we unconsciously try to keep away from as long as possible. But God does not lack the means to bring us to an unconditional surrender. He does, however, take his time. As a rule, for some considerable time we find it hard to recognize his intervention, especially when it cuts across our own activities. Usually we do not at first recognize him; we do not understand what is going on, and so we respond in a totally misguided way. Instead of slowing down or even stopping the rhythm of our own activity, we may increase our speed and run ever faster. For God's action throws us off balance. Before becoming a rock on which we can build more securely and firmly, God becomes for us a stumbling block. But still, it is his power alone that will enable us, weak as we are, to do all things in him who makes us strong, but whose power can only unfold in our weakness – that is, in the passivity that is the highest form of activity, that of humble and patient surrender.

Here again the look and the word of another person are indispensable. But it has to be someone who knows both God's action and our own weakness, someone to whom it has been given to catch God in the act, as it were – a God who, in the companion's own life, writes a straight script on crooked lines. It has to be someone who is reconciled with his own insignificance and at the same time with the miracles God constantly performs, despite the makeshift arrangements by which people ever and again try to outdo God in his own field. In offering companionship the spiritual father does in fact operate in God's own domain. There especially it will be given him to forgo doing things more quickly and better than God himself would, and never to exceed the boundaries within which grace is active. Actually it should be enough for the pupil to discern the way the spiritual companion behaves toward him. The pupil would then have a vivid example of the way in which a person may be called to tune in to grace.

To co-operate with the grace of God in such a situation

also means to co-operate with the joy of a human being. This is the ultimate challenge of spiritual companionship. Increasing joy on both sides of the relationship is the best sign of success. Just as God always watches for signs of genuine joy, so the companion also looks for the joy that smoulders in the heart of his pupil. It is the joy of God in a human heart which, initially unsure of itself, in time glows through his entire being – body, heart, psyche, including the depths of spirit and soul. The moment one has found that genuine joy, either as companion or as pupil, it is enough to remain in touch with it and, with gentle stubbornness, to pursue it faithfully wherever it leads.

When God's joy dwells in the heart of the 'father' and the same joy also dwells in the heart of the 'son', everything is again possible. Then everything can be asked for and everything can be given. For God loves someone who can give with joy, the cheerful giver (2 Cor. 9:7).

8

ON SOME OF THE FRUITS OF
THE SPIRIT

WE OWE THE expression 'fruits of the Spirit' to Paul.
He it was who energetically sought to make plain to
the early Christians that they should no longer live by the
Law but by the Spirit they had just received. He accordingly
felt the need to point out a number of signs by which one
could clearly tell whether or not a person was led by the Holy
Spirit. He calls these signs 'fruits of the Spirit'. They must be
evident in everyone who lives out of the internal freedom
given by the Spirit. In Galatians 5:22-3 he offers a summary:
'The fruit of the Spirit is love, joy, peace, patience, kindness,
goodness, faithfulness, gentleness and self-control.'
   The aim of this chapter is to discuss briefly some of these
fruits. They serve as the terrain where, in the most tangible
way, we are given a chance to learn to tune in to the grace
of God. We will limit ourselves here to three – certainly not
the least important ones – joy, self-control and love.

Joy

Jesus' great purpose for us is that our heart should rejoice
and that no one should be able to take that joy from us (John
16:22). This is also the intent of all supplicatory prayer: 'Until
now you have not asked for anything in my name,' Jesus
reproached his disciples. 'Ask and you will receive, so that
your joy may be complete' (John 16:24). It was also the reason
for Jesus' coming; he came to bring life and joy. 'I came that
they may have life and have it abundantly' (John 10:10).
Even the announcement of his birth to the shepherds came

as good news and a message of joy: 'Do not be afraid; for see
– I am bringing you good news of great joy for all the people'
(Luke 2:10). And indeed, Jesus comes to bring us joy that is
complete. His coming is good news, and throughout his entire
life he does not cease to spread joy. In him the love and
goodness of God take on visible form. According to the testi-
mony of the evangelists he did everything well and everywhere
did what was good (cf. Mark 7:37). Jesus is incredibly generous to people. He heals the sick and raises the dead. He
who harms no one is a source of joy and comfort to everyone
he meets. In particular, his disciples can attach themselves to
him without difficulty. He is always with them. He lifts their
spirits when they are tired. He takes them along with him to
a quiet place where they can relax. The moment Jesus is
present, a feast begins, for he is the bridegroom who drives
away all sadness. Accordingly, all fasting then has to go. How
could they fast when the bridegroom is present (Mark 2:19)?

Sadness, or penitence which is the expression of it, is a sign
that Jesus is not yet, or is no longer, present. After Jesus'
resurrection, therefore, fasting ceases. This can be seen from
the Easter stories in the gospel where we are struck time after
time that people so readily break and eat bread (Luke 24:30,
35; John 21:9, 13). For the bridegroom is back, and a disciple
of Jesus is then immediately entitled to the hundredfold
already promised him by Jesus in this world (Mark 10:30).
And why not? According to Jesus himself, our names are all
written in heaven that we might have joy (Luke 10:20).

Still the question has to be raised – and even if we had
been eager to dodge it, it would inescapably have urged itself
on us from our own experience: Where does that joy come
from? What is its connection with the joy this world can
already give us now? It is a hard question to answer, until
we know from experience the nature of the joy which Jesus
gives. For that reason opinions on this subject differ, even
among professional theologians. Some will stress that the joy
of this world is already a foreshadowing and foretaste of the
coming joy in the Kingdom. They therefore believe that the
joy of this world may not be simply dismissed. It is, after all,
a building-block for the joy which is coming. Others stress
the necessity of renouncing the passing joy of this world, with

an eye to the joy that is coming. In the history of spirituality we encounter both directions. Some stress the continuity between what is now and what will be even better later; others accentuate the transition and the break that comes with it. For them there is no common denominator for the joy of this world and the joy of Jesus.

It is not necessary for us to render a well-balanced theological judgement on this issue. It is enough for us to able to live with our little joy and to see to it that we increasingly receive it from the hands of Jesus by way of the Holy Spirit. If we succeed in this, then something will happen with our joy, however worldly and selfish it might initially have been. The moment Jesus is involved in every one of our joys we can only grow by them. Though this seldom happens without some mishaps, they are merely the signs of growing life, hence also of a joy that strikes deeper down and flares up higher.

The same tension between today and tomorrow, between what now is and then passes, and what comes later and always remains, can also be found in the gospel. There we are continually told of joy, and yet we cannot escape the impression that today's joy always carries its own limitation with it, and that soon everything comes to an end. The perfect and complete joy of which Jesus speaks is not simply continuous with the joys the world gives us. It is not as if we can walk from the one joy to the other without undergoing anything upsetting, even world-shaking. It is simply a fact that the kingdom of Jesus is not of this world (John 18:36), even though seed has already been sown and has mysteriously grown.

In the life of Jesus and that of his disciples there frequently occur moments when they come to a dead end. We could call them 'times in the wilderness'. For example, Jesus preaches the Word, and not without success. A fairly large crowd of people show up who believe his Word and, full of enthusiasm, follow him for two, three, even four days, to some forsaken little place in the wilderness. This goes on until suddenly it dawns on everyone that it is almost nightfall, that the crowd is hungry, and that there is no food left to feed them with. Still, their trust is not misplaced; Jesus multiplies the four loaves that they have. Nothing is more calculated to cause a new blaze of enthusiasm in a crowd that wants to proclaim him king. Jesus is on the threshold of political success. But at precisely this moment he withdraws and disappears, for he cannot take that road. His kingdom is elsewhere, outside the boundaries of this success and this happiness which the world can offer him and his disciples. Not that it is totally of the evil one. For a moment Jesus does accept this success. He lets it happen; to a certain extent he even makes use of it in the service of the Word. And earthly success can briefly promote the proclamation of the good news, just briefly. At the decisive moment when it seems everyone, including Jesus, will fall for earthly success, he is lifted up out of his earthly joy toward something very different, something that sounds very strange to our ears, so strange that even Peter, at the first announcement of coming suffering, openly protested. It is in a similar way that the Easter-experience presents itself. At first this appears to be the complete failure and the end of all joy. Jesus dies to the world in order to return full of joy to the Father, leaving to us only a vague promise that some day he will return.

The connection between Jesus and our worldly joy is not easy to recover this way. Wanting to follow Jesus in his joy, we are constantly beset by the inclination to stray and, within the sphere of his great joy which continues to charm us, to pursue limited little joys and thus in time to lose our way. It is as if every joy has to move on in a spiral, ever further toward a centre. It is assumed that we shall follow the circular movements of the spiral as best we can. But over and over there are moments in which we are tempted to move off at a tangent, breaking out of the spiral and going off by ourselves. The danger is that we then stray from the kingdom of God which is to be found in the centre of the spiral and get lost temporarily or permanently in our little human pleasures. Here another question arises: Must we then forsake happiness in order to be able to follow Jesus? And if so, to what degree? Or conversely, do not repentance and mortification mean that by following Jesus we push on to the fullness of joy (cf. John 15:11)? Just as there is a love that loves to the end, even through death (John 13:1), would there not also, by way of the same death and resurrection, be a joy that rejoices to the end?

Before we discuss this further it is a good idea to emphasize that real joy does not have to do primarily with a feeling of exuberance. We must not confuse joy with its various expressions on different levels: there is pleasure, a sense of being comfortable, an intellectual or artistic delight, deep satisfaction over work done or a successful undertaking; there are in particular the countless joys of human relationships, including the delight of love which will normally exert a lifelong hold in the life of a person. Still these are merely forms of experience. The greater they are, the deeper they will strike root in us. Real joy is very deep-rooted and we have to dig down deeply within ourselves to bring something of it to the surface. This must be the meaning of the expression we may use spontaneously when we speak of being very happy: 'I am deeply happy.' For that reason all great happiness is 'speechless'. It cannot be voiced. It is inexpressible. It seldom comes to the surface and we can never show it off. We are 'inhabited' by our joy, somewhere close to the roots of our being.

Joy is the seed-bed in which all life strikes root in order to be able to manage its own existence. Without joy we cannot live or, rather, we cannot survive. Joy wells up, especially at extraordinary moments in which we may experience our own reality or the beauty of life. Think of the joy that art can furnish, 'a thing of beauty is a joy for ever'. In the enjoyment of art genuine delight arises in us precisely because through it we can discover and, as it were, touch the very essence of people and things. It is not something we observe in the usual way through the senses, nor something that can be verbalized – this deep reality in others and in ourselves. Thus joy is always a sign that we have been granted a deeper sense of communion with 'being' or 'existence' itself.

Accordingly, joy increases in the measure that our being is growing. Joy is a mark of being alive and of progressing, moving from a being that is developing toward more being. Therefore joy is always characterized by something dynamic. It is bound up with the dynamics of people and things. In joy there is a hidden rhythm, and it is important for our own development that we attempt to coincide with this rhythm. Thus the joy that is at the root of our being ever propels us onward. It is joy's own task to pull us up to a better level of being than we now 'enjoy'. Only joy can do this.

In all vital growth fresh joy bubbles up. The clearest example of this is the joy associated with being a father or mother. It begins with sexual intercourse, the pleasure of which is designed to become a sign of a joy and a love that surpasses the ordinary human level. Wherever a human being acts creatively, a new and unheard-of joy wells up in him or her. In that way joy is also associated with what happens in a person in the process of spiritual growth, especially when he or she is given new life from God. Here occurs the deep joy of repentance, when God recreates us in his forgiving love. This is undoubtedly one of the most striking existential moments in our lives, being touched by God's mercy in order to be allowed to live in him. It happens also in friendship; there we are accepted by the other in our deepest being, a being that, though still concealed from ourselves, has been recognized by the other's love. In genuine friendship the encounter between two people no longer holds any threat; we can be ourselves at a much deeper level than the parts of us that appear on the surface. For that reason we can say of friendship that we 'enjoy' it; that is, it supports us and helps us in developing our best selves.

Accordingly, joy is a mark of being, to the extent that it grows in us and is in the process of surpassing its own boundaries. In a sense our joy always lies a little beyond where we are today. It is a summons, a challenge. It anticipates the joy of further growth in relationship, either with another person or with God. But precisely to the measure in which joy pushes us ever further along the spiral of happiness, there is also the possibility of deviation and getting lost in another happiness. On the road of joy we often encounter a kind of crossroads, where a possibility occurs of going off at a tangent toward a limited, little happiness in which we run the danger of getting stuck. Not that this little happiness comes from the devil. Not at all! Yet it is no longer today's joy, the joy that corresponds to our own deep rhythm. Even if this small happiness were of great value, it would separate us from our inner dynamism;

without it we would be further ahead, closer to the primal joy that is at the centre of the spiral. For to live is to grow and to grow ever further. To live is to develop; and life that no longer develops is dead. Consequently, real life is always somehow in the process of tearing itself free, deepening the birth experience. It has to do with labour pains and the joy of giving birth.

The only ascesis that may therefore be 'imposed' on joy is that which lies locked in its own rhythm. It is the movement of the spiral which increasingly distances itself from the outer circles and curves around to the inner core. The ascesis of joy is therefore the nature of joy itself. Real joy, like real love, brings its own purification with it. To purify joy one never needs to put constraints on it from the outside; to pursue the joy on its own path we need only to revolve along with the spiral, and we will not be able to escape the purification. It is inherent in the joy itself. To keep real joy we must continually be detached from what are merely its provisional forms of expression. We have to be prepared at every moment to let go of a limited happiness to be able to thrust through to a deeper inner joy, to the extremity of joy that always coincides with the extremity of love.

If we have to speak of ascesis or penitence, it can only be in the service of greater joy. Penitence is never an attack on joy, as though every joy should be under suspicion and be experienced only with a bad conscience, as though every joy had to be pruned or curtailed from the outside. Ascesis is the practice of surrendering oneself to the real life and the deep joy that surges in us. Following this line of thinking, it is not so much acting against something (*agere contra*), but rather acting in accordance with (*agere secundum*) joy in harmony with our real being; or if we prefer to stress the dynamism of joy, it is a going beyond (*agere ultra*), surpassing the joy that was given only for yesterday and today.

Accordingly, genuine ascesis has little to do with will-power or energy and will never end in compulsiveness. On the contrary, ascesis is an easy and flexible kind of surrender in us, an act of relaxing and opening ourselves up, so that life can stream in and out of us without hindrance and almost without pain. It is, after all, the liberation and birth of the new human-being. In that sense ascesis involuntarily evokes the image of what we might call a 'painless delivery'. The more fearful and anxious a young mother is, the more effort she makes and unwittingly works against the physiological process that comes over her, the greater will be the pain of her delivery. Conversely, the more she relaxes, the more she yields to the ripe fruit of the life that is making its way through her body, and the more readily she surrenders to the joy of becoming a mother, the better chance she has of a painless delivery.

A painless delivery is the most suitable image for ascesis, one that speaks simultaneously of joy and of penitence. It conveys the only ascesis that is consistent with the Christian perspective, ascesis that is based on, and yields to, joy. The measure of ascesis then will be the measure of the joy that prevails, if it is to be really painless, joyful penitence (*Perfectae Caritatis 7**). We are after all dealing with the life of Jesus that has to come to birth in us, that has to push a path through our bodies and hearts in order to win over our entire being.

The image of a 'painless'† delivery was also used by Jesus when he spoke of the unavoidable pain that would become the source of a deep, definitive joy:

> In all truth I tell you,
> you will be weeping and wailing
> while the world will rejoice;
> you will be sorrowful,
> but your sorrow will turn to joy.
> A woman in childbirth suffers,
> because her time has come;
> but when she has given birth to the child she forgets
>   the suffering
> in her joy that a human being has been born into the
>   world.
> So it is with you: you are sad now,

---

*The conciliar decree on the renewal of religious life, *The Way*, 1966, 1968.
†I have put 'painless' in quotation marks here because in the same breath the author speaks of 'the unavoidable pain' that accompanies childbirth. He clearly means to relativize the pain in view of the joy that normally arises from the experience of childbirth. *Translator.*

> but I shall see you again, and your hearts will be
>   full of joy,
> and that joy no one shall take from you.
>
> (John 16:20–2 NJB)

A woman giving birth suffers on account of the life that has grown in her body, but at the same time she is full of joy because of the child whose mother she will be. As the moment of birth approaches, although actual pain may increase, her suffering will lessen as she is able to yield gratefully to her joy and to the life that is born of her.

Every disciple of Jesus, in whom the life of Jesus must ever take clearer shape, is like that woman giving birth, given over to the pain and to the joy of growth. He, or she, lives from within that joy; that is, from within the form and full stature of Jesus Christ toward whom he is always growing, from within what he will be tomorrow. His ascesis is therefore always a joyful ascesis and the only measure of his ascesis is to be found in the joy that is given him by the Holy Spirit. Does not Saint Benedict tell us in his Rule that every extraordinary ascesis or mortification has value only to the degree that it is offered to God 'in the joy of the Holy Spirit' (*Rule*, ch. 49, 6). It is important therefore that every disciple of Jesus clings to his joy. There are two ways in which a person can fail to do justice to that joy and to the life of God within him. He may aim higher than the joy he has in fact been given; he can also remain below the level of the joy intended for him.

The first way is to will to do one's best without joy. It is to perform a kind of ascesis in the wrong sense of the word: ascesis not guided by the inner prodding of the Holy Spirit of which joy is the palpable fruit. Before God such ascesis is of no value whatever. It is a pagan business often deeply interwoven with self-sufficiency and pride. Here too is room for masochistic tendencies that find satisfaction in questionable penitential practices. It all has little to do with grace and is at best a sign of good will, a kind of good will that God does not leave unanswered, to be sure, but that he really does not look for. Pagan ascesis causes us to aim at a level much higher than has actually been given us in the joy of the Spirit.

In the long run it could quench that joy in us and even dull
our spiritual sensitivity.

A more frequent and likely occurrence, however, is that we
would do less than justice to the grace of God and the life of
Jesus in us because we aim at a level lower than the joy that
was given us. From fear of the pain that comes with every
growth process we then remain stuck in a limited and small
form of happiness. This happiness can even be a spiritual joy
– consolation in prayer or success in the 'cure of souls'. For
we can also become stuck in a spiritual joy, so that it keeps
us from thrusting on toward a deeper level of joy. For that
reason it is good if from time to time we have the boldness to
pray for the ability to discover that deep joy in ourselves or,
better still, to pray that at some point it may take a hold of
us. Ascesis only buoys us up when it is totally attuned to joy.
Then the need to cling to a small and transient happiness
shrivels away. It is Jesus' own joy that takes hold of us and
takes us along with him through every mortification and death
to his resurrection and new life.

Turning inward and being silent

The silence that is associated with inwardness and self-control, is especially an area where we get onto the wavelength
of grace. Only grace can draw us inward in order to quieten
down in the presence of the Word of God and wordlessly to
express our deepest being and that of the whole world before
God. For that matter, maintaining silence always has to do
with a word. It is either attuned to the word we have to take
in, or it is the space in which we gain the ability to utter it.

Before silence can be these things, however, it is ambiguous.
Silence may be the expression of impotence and sin, but also
of fullness and fruitfulness. In Genesis, before the fall, Adam
is the speaking person *par excellence*. In speech he even actively
participates in creation. God himself invited him to name all
the creatures and in his very own person came to speak with
man at the time of the evening breeze (Gen. 3:8). That dialogue was broken by sin. The next time God appeared for
that evening walk Adam and Eve shrank back in shame. They
no longer dared to speak to God. But also true dialogue broke

off between the two of them. Eve was to tempt Adam and Adam was to accuse his wife before God. Their word conveyed no longer love but impotence and hatred. In future it not only carried blessing but was also capable of cursing. The confusion of language at Babel is a clear reflection of the fragmentation that now prevails among people; the multiplicity of their languages is a great hindrance to mutual understanding. But also in man himself there is now dichotomy and confusion. He is no longer able to be honest in his speech. He has become a liar and by his tongue he can now violate the truth. For out of the abundance of the heart the mouth speaks, as Jesus put it (Matt. 12:33–7). Now, that heart has become evil. For that reason too, the word is now ambiguous. It can do good as well as evil. It is an instrument with which we can 'bless' God and injure our brother, writes James in an important passage in which he stresses all the dangers of the tongue (Jas. 3:1–12).

Thus one reason to handle words with care and perhaps to maintain silence clearly emerges: our impotence and our poverty. It is better to keep silent, for in speech one takes a risk. Did not Jesus himself say that his disciples would have to give an account for every word they spoke and be condemned for every careless word they uttered (Matt. 12:36, 37)? This is a pronouncement which simultaneously underscores the great value as well as the ambiguity of the spoken word. This first form of maintaining silence does not seem very positive. Still, we often need it more than we think. It is well for us to live as wounded people who know their wounds and show by their entire attitude that they look for healing.

Maintaining silence out of impotence is also possible between God and us, especially during prayer. This is not yet the silence that seizes us from within when suddenly the Word of God lights up in our heart. On the contrary, it is a silence which proceeds from the great distance which separates us from God. Still, it is silence full of the hope and expectation which genuinely and deeply purify us. We believe that at some point God will say no more about our sins and purely out of grace will give us a sign. Our wordlessness expresses both this intense expectancy and our need to say clearly that we are not yet satisfied. It is the silence of the beggar who will not stop holding out his hand, an act involving a refusal and rejection of all that could distract one from God. The genuinely poor are convinced that only God can act savingly and that only his Word can accomplish miracles.

What this miracle could turn out to be is already visible in the earthly life of Jesus. Jesus came to earth not so much to be silent as to restore the dialogue between God and man that had been broken. It is he who comes to remove from our heart the dissonance that makes it so difficult for us to arrive at true dialogue with God. Jesus does this the more readily because he is himself God and man. As God, he is the living and perfect Word of the Father which we may clearly hear in him. As God, Jesus is also the answer to the Father so that, himself human, he can best restore the human response.

First, Jesus is the Word which the Father addresses to us. This is clear from the Father's words at the Transfiguration: 'This is my son, my Beloved; listen to him!' (Luke 9:35). In fact, Jesus often pointed out that he is merely the Word of the Father. Being sent by the Father, he can only pass on what he had received from the Father. To the Jews who were amazed that he ventured to act as teacher he said frankly: 'My teaching is not mine but his who sent me' (John 7:16). For Jesus to be able to say this presupposes in him an intense openness and devotion to the Father that is a form of silence and inwardness. For him to be the Word of the Father, Jesus has to be, in all his humanity, total silence and attentiveness toward the Father. To be the sounding board for what the Father wants to communicate, Jesus has to exercise a high degree of self-control, an essential listening posture totally attuned to the Father. Jesus in his full humanity can be the Word of God because present, deep in his being, there is a fathomless silence.

At the same time, however, Jesus is man's response to God. In his silence and his speech the dialogue, broken by Adam, is again restored. Paul pithily articulates these two aspects of Jesus' being Word in 2 Corinthians 1:19-20:

> For the Son of God, Jesus Christ, whom we proclaimed among you . . . was not 'Yes' and 'No', but in him it is always 'Yes'. For in him every one of God's promises is

a 'Yes'. For this reason it is through him that we say the
'Amen' to the glory of God.

Precisely because Jesus is so selflessly and transparently the
Word of the Father he has also been the best affirmative
answer of man. He was the first 'Amen', to which in every
liturgy we can gratefully give our assent and which we can
jubilantly applaud: Amen, Alleluia! Thus the essential and
boundless silence of Jesus' humanity was filled to the brim
with humanity's assent (the 'yes-word'), with the Amen of
the heavenly and earthly liturgy. Is not this Amen the name
John gives to Jesus in the Apocalypse: 'I am the Amen' (3:14)?
To be able to continue saying, and to be this Amen Jesus
had, at a given moment, to give himself up to death so as to
reach the utmost: endorsement of the Word, the Will, and the
Love of the Father. 'Not my will but your will be done' (Mark
14:36). At this decisive moment Jesus' human will had fallen
silent and come to complete rest. To this day, all believing
silence has been woven around these words of Jesus. The
reason is that we need time and rest, in order to pronounce
these words in all humility before the Father; and also that
at a given moment these words are for ever adequate for us:
Amen! Alleluia!

To grow inwardly

From the above it is clear not only that there are different
motivations for silence but also that we cannot simply, from
the beginning, practise exterior or interior silence on our own
and without risk. Inwardness is accompanied by spiritual
development. Genuine silence will be the outcome of a gradual
growth process.

   To consider this point a little further, we may reflect for a
moment on a period in life when we maintained an intense
silence and at the same time lived intensely, where rapid
growth coincided with speechlessness. It was the time before
and after birth when we could not yet speak. This period of
enforced speechlessness was a gradual process of discovering
the word we would at some point stammer out to father or
mother. Still this silence was very relative; despite everything,

the contact we had with our parents was, from the very first moment, very intense. There was constant interaction and growth in experience. During the first few days after birth, contact was mediated by the body and the skin. Quite soon we recognized our father and mother with our eyes. From then on there was 'eye-language' between parents and baby. A few weeks later the next step occurred, the smile. By smiling we showed we recognized our father and mother and confirmed the tie between us.

While still a baby we could already absorb their words and to a degree understand them. The first word we discovered for ourselves and could claim as our own was for 'mother' or 'father'. It contained both affirmation and appeal that had ripened in the long silence. Even then it was already the best expression of ourselves as we felt taken up into the love and care of our parents. This had taken us months of silence. It was nothing other than a slow and patient process of digging out that new possibility in us. Perhaps it had to do with struggle and pain. The first fruit of this effort was a word of love, a loaded word, a real word. Much later, the moment we grasped the language, we in turn were taken by surprise by words. They became too much for us. It was no longer so real and so healthy. We knew from experience how a person could use words that were not in keeping with his own truth and behind which he could hide. Every person can become a liar, as words become a defence mechanism, a way of reacting against a fellow human being, oneself, or sometimes God. Words can degenerate into formalism and convention, and become a mask that is our undoing.

Thinking about these possibilities we again yearn for silence, be it at first the silence of impotence. At this point it is only a discipline I impose on myself to block the road to this superficial disguise with which I deceive my self and others. Exterior silence, for it to be fruitful, has to do still more. It is designed to put me in the way of the yearning that throbs in me, concealed beneath the noise of words, of the interior self where the source of real silence is located. Some day we shall have the privilege of pushing through to this innermost part of ourselves, where another father is waiting for us, the Father from whom all fatherhood on earth takes its name (Eph. 3:15), and whose name we may try to utter. Deep within us there is a bond of love, of which the bond with father and mother we discovered in infancy is merely the sign. It is the bond with the Father, in the Son, and through the Spirit. For it is the Spirit who haltingly teaches us to say, 'Abba, Father' (Rom. 8:15). Past the silence, that is now a fullness of love, we again stammer out the same word, the first word we uttered as a human being.

Now arises the interplay between the silence we impose on ourselves from without and the interior silence or inwardness which we are now beginning to recognize as an inexpressible 'happening' deep within us. This interplay is not immediately complete. Gradually the inwardness takes over the role of the exterior silence. For the latter is called to become inwardness. It is a silence that breathes life because it *is* life, interior life, spiritual life, eternal life; it is, as Isaac the Syrian put it, the language of the world to come.

To promote that inwardness not only exterior silence but also interior silence is needed. The latter is much more important, and unfortunately also less familiar than the former. For our interior world is not of itself attuned to God, except for the deep core where we may accept our existence from the hands of God. That core, however, is surrounded by a screen of desires and thoughts that do not directly set our feet on the path to God. Like our body, so our inwardness still bears the marks of sin. Therefore, an interior vigilance is needed, so that we do not yield to whatever thought or desire announces itself. A certain poverty or sobriety of thought and desires will free or scoop out within us a deep inner emptiness into which the life of the Spirit within us will bubble up, like an unstoppable spring of water, from the bottom of our heart. Perhaps the idea of the spring is a good image for the silence, one which always has to do with the Spirit. Jesus himself uses it:

> Let anyone who is thirsty come to me, and let the one who believes in me drink. As the scripture has said, 'Out of the believer's heart shall flow rivers of living water.' Now he said this about the Spirit, which believers in him were to receive. (John 7:37–9).

Silence and inwardness are nothing other than the Holy Spirit creating an emptiness which will become the deep space where the spring can bubble up within us. That spring is the Spirit himself. For we are born of water and Spirit (John 3:5). It is water that bubbles up in us the moment silence makes room for it. Then there is no need to dig. Genuine interior silence cuts out the silence that is imposed from outside. Water digs out its own channels. One only has to let it flow.

A humble love

Nothing so vividly expresses the character of a human being as his or her capacity to love. It is equally clear that this capacity is not immediately 'on hand'. Only after many years of maturing, perhaps a life-time, does one consciously begin to develop gradually the capacity to love that lies locked up within. In this context one's spiritual experience and development play an important role. Ultimately love has to do with God, for God is love, and we can love only to the degree we have been given the experience of God's love and grace.

A recurrent theme in this book has been that our connection with grace is given to us in the context of temptation and conversion. There we encounter the overwhelming mercy of God. To the degree that all love must also be the fruit of the Holy Spirit within us, this experience of impotence and of mercy will, in the moment of conversion, also have an effect on our capacity to enter into contact with others out of love. For in this process a love is released in us that takes us much further than our natural love could manage. Our love then begins to resemble the love of the Father who is in heaven, of which Jesus himself testified that he makes his sun rise on the evil and on the good (Matt. 5:45). Love will then even take us to the point where Jesus asks it to extend itself not only to those who love us – for pagans do this also – but even to those who hate us, our enemies (Matt. 5:44). It is a tall order, one that becomes impossible the moment we have to rely merely on personal magnanimity. Only long association with grace, or rather its long association with us – in its patience and generosity, its being simultaneously tender and tough – teaches us over and over how to love better.

In the present climate we again have to deal with elements that make it difficult to speak of love as spiritual experience. First there is the fact that until recently many people did not know how to handle emotional love. Meanwhile, much has been said and written, but it is not certain that changes have actually evolved as rapidly as the flood of words and writings would lead one to think. Well-intended but loud proclamations are usually not enough to inculcate a warm heart in a person. As a rule the urgency with which a given issue is discussed betrays the uneasiness that still governs us.

At this point I do not intend to expand on this topic. I do, however, want to say a word about a double malformation of love that we often encounter nowadays, and that goes back perhaps to the way earlier generations viewed emotional love. The first distortion is seen when love is twisted into active service. This says that in order to love it is not important to feel anything but to start doing something. The second distortion results in one-sidedly stressing the social aspects of love at the expense of the personal ones. One is asked to love a nation, a class, or a good cause, rather than the individual person one unexpectedly encounters. What has such a double shift to do with love?

Of course I do not mean to say that love will not lead us to pitch in to help those who really need it. I only mean that at the start, for me really to love, it is important that I feel a sense of need myself. My own need for love plays a role as great as the material or even the spiritual needs of others. Although at first this sounds selfish, it is not so really. If I start too quickly to serve others and to do things for them, I am skipping the important stage of friendship. That stage is perhaps even essential. It is possible that, unconsciously, I am very eager to leave this out, because it is really much easier to do something for others than to let the other approach me as someone I myself need.

In love it is essential that I first be inwardly wounded by the other. I must give him time to wound me. A need will then arise in me that can only be alleviated by the other. To love is to say to someone, You are my joy; I cannot live without you; I need you. Love awakens a deep need, makes a person needy and poor, and even dependent on another.

Love makes us open up to the other, teaches us to listen, makes us receptive. In this sense love can never be without genuine humility. It is especially love that makes me humble in relation to the one for whom I so intensely long. For most people this is perhaps the most difficult aspect of friendship – not so much the emotional love from which some people would run, but the fact that love would lead us to recognize that we really and critically need the other, that only he can give us something to the degree that we give ourselves to him. We can understand that many people unconsciously resist something that might be considered weak or cowardly, and that they will do everything they can to escape this trial. An active, generous service to others is the most obvious way to do this, one moreover that flatters our self-love. A so-called altruistic love may be a way to avoid love, particularly the genuine humility that is an ingredient of love. It is rather easy to be a hero in the love of one's neighbour. (Does this sound strange? But the idea is not hard to accept.) Nevertheless, external heroism has little to do with genuine love, love that entails vulnerability and weakness. Accordingly, we do not speak of the heroes of friendship, or of a heroic married life. Love does not need heroism; it could be devastating to love. Love is love and is sufficient to itself. Similarly, real love is enough for us to be at our best.

Another way to escape being confronted with our weakness in love is to focus it solely on groups. We devote our energies to our colleagues (in the plural!), to our parish to the Church, to our country, to underdeveloped countries. As with absent-mindedness, we overlook the real person. It is easier to love in the plural – with an abstract and idealized love that does not injure either ourselves or others, but that also does not actually do anyone any good. In this way we can be very active for distant 'neighbours' in faraway foreign lands and at war with all our colleagues at home. Again, this is a way to exempt ourselves from real love, love that always operates in the singular. You do not love a group but first and foremost another individual person, someone who may hurt you, with whom you may lose face, and to whom you may also be able to accord the honour of being the only one who can at a given time meet your need.

This capacity for being wounded by love, this weakness which surfaces in every love relationship, is something we can learn only from God and his grace. In his redemptive activities he has left us a paradigm of love and we know from experience how he works with us every day. Did he not so love the world that he gave his only Son to it (John 3:16)? And the Son – did he not say that he would leave the ninety-nine other sheep in the wilderness in order, as the good Shepherd, to go after the lost sheep and, full of joy, to bring it back to the fold carrying it on his shoulders (Luke 15:4)? And is not he himself the Father who stands by the gate every day looking out for the lost son in order, the moment he sees him in the distance, to run to him to be the first to embrace him (Luke 15:20)? And when, the night before his passion, he wanted to give a sign of love 'to the end', was it not also he who removed his upper garment and, as a servant, knelt before his disciples (including Judas) to wash their feet (John 13:5)? God was so vulnerable before humans, he felt such a need for them, and the price he was prepared to pay for them so great, that ultimately there can be no greater joy in heaven than the joy which only a sinner can create in the heart of God when he turns back to God in penitence (Luke 15:7). God's love never shatters us; on the contrary, it is on the human scale – gentle, humble, and grateful.

Humble love (*humilis caritas*) is perhaps the greatest of all evangelical virtues, much more rare than the frequent use of the word 'love' in contemporary literature would lead us to suspect. Love in the image of God – generous, patient, gentle love toward everyone, toward those nearest and those most distant, toward friend and enemy, toward just anyone who shows up. A Cistercian abbot who lived in the twelfth century, the blessed Guerric of Igny, said it in his way: 'It is the property of friendship to make itself small before its friends' (*Proprium est amicitae humiliari pro amicis*).

Such people are a great blessing to the Church and to the world. As a rule they are easy to recognize. For real love attracts and wins others – without knowing it. Sometimes they live in obscurity and isolation, but one word from them, uttered on the threshold of their hermitage, can be enough to lift you out of your saddle, like Paul, and to let you have a taste of the grace of God.

I should like to conclude this chapter on the fruits of the Spirit with a personal recollection of a pilgrimage to some hermits on Mount Athos. Actually there is not much to say. I only have to confess that in my imagination I had formed a totally different picture of them – as likely to be a wild and hard people, heroes of ascesis and isolation and incapable of much human contact. The reality was precisely the opposite. Seldom had I been privileged to experience such love, a gentle, humble love, by which I immediately felt taken up into their prayer and carried along to God. Seldom, also, have I felt closer to people, somewhere in the deep heart of the world that never stops beating for God. Alas, so few people have any inkling of this love.

9

GROWING IN GRACE
THROUGH PRAYER

REPEATEDLY, IN PRECEDING chapters, mention of grace has led us involuntarily into the subject of prayer. It could hardly be otherwise. After all, in the course of praying we are constantly working with grace or, rather, grace is working with us. To pray is to learn to tune in to grace. In this final chapter my aim is to illuminate certain aspects of this.

A word on prayer

It may be useful first to make clear what is meant here by prayer. For there are many forms of prayer: spoken prayer and silent prayer; exterior prayer and interior prayer; liturgical prayer and private prayer. In the wake of the charismatic movement new forms of prayer have become available; for example, praying in tongues.

I do not intend here to make a choice or to express a preference. There are, after all, many possible roads to prayer. The only important thing is that these roads eventually bring persons to a point where deep prayer wells up in them. Every form of prayer must issue in this genuine deep prayer. Prayer presupposes that something happens to the person who prays (the pray-er). It is always a real happening in the most vital sense of the word 'event'. It is a prayer-event.

Precisely what happens in prayer? For the time being I shall not attempt to define prayer, seeking first to approach the event from the outside with the aid of a number of familiar images. By means of images and living symbols I can perhaps suggest more than concepts could.

In the first place prayer has something to do with a *surprise attack*. The person who surprises us, however, is not a stranger, an outsider, but rather an 'insider'. We feel taken by surprise by something or someone in us who has been with us a long time, whom we have unwittingly carried with us, but who now suddenly surfaces, as it were, and comes to lay claim to us. We are seized by him, or her. Initially this insider seems strange to us. But very quickly we sense that he actually belongs to us, that he is even another side, a still unfamiliar side, of our own ego. Not a dark side but a light side. Not the dormant but the dynamic side, a source of power, of violence, of life. It is our deepest and best side, our eternal side that presents itself.

A second image that may convey something of the prayer-event is that of *becoming conscious*. To pray is to wake up to something that has long remained unconscious. In the life of every human being there is a long period of unconscious prayer. It was there but we did not know it. To pray, then, is to allow this unconscious prayer to become conscious in us. This becoming conscious of something that has been unconscious is always an important step in every human life, as in every therapy. For therapy is the technique of letting something of the unconscious in us rise to the surface. First we are confronted by it. We must accept and absorb it in order later, in a balanced way, to integrate it into our daily life, into our conduct, into our thinking, and loving, and achieving peace. Prayer is the unconscious divine side that becomes conscious and that must be quietly integrated in our life.

Another image for depicting the prayer-event is that of a *spring*, a spring that has long been blocked by a stone. It is there but temporarily sealed off, blocked. When the stone is taken away the water spurts up. For it is living water, according to the image Jesus used to describe the life of the Spirit within us (John 4:10). Water bubbles up without effort. It is also power; it sustains, propels, scoops out channels. A lot can happen when a dike breaks and water floods everything behind it.

A dike that breaks. The prayer-event also has to do with a

sudden *break-through*, something that breaks into the open (
is thrown open. It is simultaneously something violent and
something very delicate, something of which we then prefer
to say that it unfolds and blossoms. Still, it has something to
do with the overpowering rush of a mighty pentecostal wind.
In his lyrical medieval Dutch, Jan van Ruysbroek sang of
prayer as an *orewoet*, an irresistible hurricane. In the face of
such a storm we can only surrender ourselves, drop our
weapons, and let it happen.

Finally, we can also liken prayer to *birth*, the coming into
the world of new life. A birth is accompanied by labour pains
but also by a deep joy, because a new human being is entering
the world. Prayer-events are always a new birth – a deep
life with which we have long been pregnant, that has been
germinating and growing within us, suddenly and sometimes
startlingly emerges into the open.

What is the nature of this up-until-now unfamiliar life of
which one suddenly becomes conscious, this new human being
that emerges, this unconscious side of our being that now
becomes conscious? The answer to this question is the same
for all mystics. Prayer is the awakening in us of our deepest
reality, of the point in our being where – somewhere unknown,
unseen, unfelt – we are in touch with God; or rather, where
we are touched every moment by the creative activity of God.
Byzantine writers sometimes called it the *topos tou Theou*, the
place where God is present in our being. The only difference
among mystics concerns the name each gives to that place:
nous, *mens*, *cor*, the foundation of our being, the core, the
depths, the abyss of the soul, *sommet de l'âme* (the summit of
the soul), *cîme de l'esprit* (the top of the spirit). Some verses
written by Gezelle* suggest themselves to me at this point:

> I'm far from You,
> though You,
> sweet source of all that is alive
> or ever makes alive,
> draw nearer to me than all else

---

*Guido Gezelle (1830–99), Flemish poet-priest, whose poetry was character-
ized by simplicity, piety and union with nature. *Translator*.

> and send, dear sun,
> Your all-pervasive rays
> down into my deepest depths.

God, in the process of creating, touches us all, as he does in
Michelangelo's painting of the creation of Adam. The Father's
finger just catches Adam's finger, never again to let go of it
– else Adam, and we all, would perish. Here the question
arises: Is it possible to locate this creative contact between
God and ourselves somewhere in the human consciousness?

In the process of recreating us God touches us much more
deeply in the Son who dwells with and within us, in the Spirit
who was poured into our heart and whose sighs or groaning
deep within us precede each of our own prayers long before
we consciously start praying ourselves. The Pauline passages
are perfectly clear on this point (Rom. 8:26). Again the question arises: Is the prayer that is granted us in advance percep-
tible? Can it make itself conscious? If so, whereabouts within
us does it occur?

Prayer in weakness

The answer to this question is not easy. Our experience of
prayer is usually limited and rather unhappy. At times it will
even be profoundly inadequate. We then sense that we do not
really know how to pray. Although we have tried out various
ways, in most cases it was futile.

Some people make great use of their imagination. They
try to evoke scenes from the gospel or images from current
iconography. This is not wrong. In this connection a distinct
place must certainly be accorded to the icon of Jesus, either
from the East or from the West, the sacred Face of the Saviour,
la Sainte Face, the sacramental sign of the glorified Lord. Just
as in the Bible God left his Word to us in the form of human
words, so we also get to see something of his invisible Being
in the human features of the Face of Jesus. 'Whoever has seen
me has seen the Father' (John 14:9). According to age-old
tradition, something of the features of Jesus has remained
visible, and the spiritual power of the mystery of salvation
has been preserved, in Christian art. Hence the important

role which icons and altar-pieces played in the liturgy and in spiritual experience – at least until recently. In the ossification of the liturgy before Vatican II, a process paralleled by the separate development of the visual arts in the West (many refer to it as a crisis), we have suffered a severe loss.

However this may be, we merely want here to emphasize that it is precisely the power that inheres in the icon – or *sacra imago*, in the Western idiom – that enables the spectator to go beyond the image as such or his own imagination. It is through the image that our heart is struck, just as also the Word of God in the Bible does not speak primarily to our intellect but must pierce our heart. It is very important, therefore, that the use of images does not cause us to linger in the imagination. Images also have the capacity to distract us from the essential. For example, though I have made a pilgrimage to the Holy Land and now again attempt during prayer to picture the holy places, I can never be sure that I get any further than the memories of an instructive journey I undertook a few years back. But am I getting into the presence of Jesus? That is the question.

Every image, for that matter, is designed to bring us to an experience. What experience? Perhaps we are attempting, with the aid of an image, to arouse an assortment of feelings, feelings of joy, love, trust, gratitude? To some degree this can always be done. We can even revel in those feelings, find personal satisfaction in them. We may also get bored in record time – perhaps not the first time around, but then the second or third time. Feelings are not inexhaustible. They are limited, very dependent on moods, much more than on good intentions or on what resembles spiritual longings. Even if a person were to have a reasonable degree of success because he has at his disposal a rich emotional life, where is he? Is it God who wounds him, who strikes him deep in his emotional life, when he is so hard at work stirring up his feelings, just as he would do with glowing embers that threaten to go out? Before long he is satisfied, not because he is deficient in generosity or perseverance, but only in virtue of the fact that his feelings are not inexhaustible. Only God is inexhaustible in us. But how do we find our way to God?

Others believe the rational way is more likely to succeed.

They give free rein to their intellect. The traditional term 'reflection' and 'meditation' also point in that direction. In the worst case, the reference is to reflection on abstract truths; in the best, to reflection on the words of Scripture.

In both cases, however, it is still primarily a reflective activity whose aim is to arrive at clearer insight or firmer convictions, and on that basis again to stir up one's emotions. The words of Scripture are not primarily designed to be weighed intellectually. They are meant to pierce us and to open up our inmost being. They speak primarily to the heart, not to our intellect. If they reach only our intellect, then meditation becomes something like an encouraging pat on the back in the sense of: 'You can really tell that we were right, so just continue to do your best!' I am exaggerating a little to show how in this way, too, we may slip rapidly toward a moralism of a most dubious kind. For up to now nothing has *happened*. The road is blocked and we are keeping the barriers in place. The only thing that has occurred is that we have done our very best – and it is precisely this that is unfruitful. If only we would for a moment do less than our best, we might perhaps discover the place where Jesus is waiting for us.

This place can be described as an impasse, a necessary cul-de-sac, a blind alley, a blessed dead-end; or to put it still more graphically, a street that has no end. An unavoidable and necessary impasse! To be sure, we can take the intellectual tack and so experience personally that it does not happen there; the same is true regarding our imagination or our superficial sentiments. It will have to happen some other way. The impasse must induce us for a while to exclude the ways that are so familiar to us. For we must quieten down, find a deep interior silence, and simply wait there until something else in our inner life rises to the surface. Not an idea, or feelings or image, but something else: a noiseless, feelingless, imageless, 'thoughtless' presence – not so much some*thing* else as *Someone Else*.

What I am attempting to describe here is a very important stage in prayer, a stage we are actually afraid of. The arrival of all our efforts at a dead-end brings home to us in the most personal way that we do not know how to pray at all! We

may fight this realization and in every possible way increase
our efforts by being more virtuous, more devout, more
involved with and for others. All this is actually easier than
letting our deep impotence before God sink in.

What can we do in the impasse? The answer is simple: stay
in it. That is, under no pretext should we run from it. For
there, at the very place of our futile efforts, we must be *saved*
from the impasse, *healed* of our impotence. The passive form
of the verb, 'to be saved', is essential here. The idea is not
that we must rescue ourselves, but that we must *be* rescued
by someone else. This means we must learn to yield totally –
to remain stuck, as it were, in our impotence – in order from
that 'vantage point', and from nowhere else, to be taken up
into God's power. For prayer, too, falls within the compass
of the experience of salvation. It has to become a real-life
illustration of what Paul said: 'Whenever I am weak, then I
am strong, for the power of God is only manifest in weakness'
(2 Cor 12:10).

This may sometimes be a long process. It is a matter of
progressively learning to surrender ourselves. Our own effort
at prayer must gradually, almost imperceptibly but certainly,
be taken up into and, as it were, dissolved in God's action.
Now God takes the initiative and we let him do it. We surrender ourselves totally to his activity within us. Such abandon-
ment is not easy. We may actually resist it for a long time,
often with considerable stubborness, a pious zeal that is totally
superfluous and even damaging. God, who knows us better
than we know ourselves, may for a while let us go on like
that, allowing us to defend ourselves against him. Sometimes
he will even, for a little while, let us entertain the notion that
we are making progress in prayer this way.

Actually God is asking something painful of us. Without
any explanation he comes to take prayer out of our hands.
We get the impression this way that we are about to lose
everything we thought we had so far gained. We had perhaps
made some headway on the road to prayer – at least it seemed
that way. But now that road has suddenly been blocked.
There is no longer any answer. We are straining at the leash
without any hope of change. We are not always to blame for
this, nor is it due to a lack of generosity on our part. In most

cases God intends it to be so. He seeks to convey to us that he is now waiting for us somewhere else. Prayer is still available to us but at another place, at a much deeper level. In the past we never doubted that we needed the gift of God that is called grace in order to be able to pray well. And yet we also had the impression that we had prayer somewhere within our reach. Our efforts after all had not been in vain! But now God prefers to pose the issue differently. Now the prayer to which he is inviting us is to be only from him; it is pure grace. We have no grip on it. Our sole remaining option is to open our hands and heart in order to let prayer well up as a gift from the Lord in the place where he is giving it.

To persevere in the impasse also means not scrambling back to the little byways and paths where we used to attempt prayer with some degree of success. More specifically it means not falling back on our intellect, our imagination, our feelings. For the time being all these organs will have to 'fast', to become quiet, to lie still, to be almost eliminated. The more we make noises in that area, the less our chance that prayer can break through in us; the road is occupied by something else, that stone is still covering the spring.

The word 'persevere' may still be a trifle too active to convey what has to happen at this impasse. The ancient biblical and patristic idiom here employs the verb *hypomenein* and the noun *hypomone* (literally 'to stay under something'). One could almost translate this as, to dive under in the impasse and to remain there, waiting until something else comes to surprise us.

This exclusion of all other spiritual activities usually brings about a certain darkness, a feeling of dryness, a sense of desolation, the impression of an emptiness perhaps, a dizzying depth of vacuity, sometimes also the pain of hunger and thirst. These negative feelings are actually very positive signals. They are the sign that we are already in the process of sensing the other side of our inner ego. But it is still unconscious, for we are not at all accustomed to it. It is still all very strange. Everything seems wrong. But precisely that is a good sign. By remaining in the impasse we are unwittingly getting through to somewhere. Or rather, something else now has a chance of getting through to us.

When Jesus wanted to speak about the life of the Spirit in us he used the figure of a gushing spring. It is like living water that must become in us a spring that wells up to eternal life (John 4:14). Prayer is that deep spring in us. Actually it was there all along as the breath of the Holy Spirit who was actively and unceasingly praying within us. We did not notice it. Without knowing it we had piled up numerous stones around that spring. Such a spring is subject to natural pressure. You can artificially hold back or hinder that pressure. You can also give it free course and yield to it. But even the most intense efforts can do little or nothing to increase the pressure. We must be very careful, for it could well be precisely our efforts that form the stones obstructing the natural gushing of the spring – without our knowing it!

In order to pray more and better we must often do less, let go of more things, give up numerous good intentions, and be content to yield to the inner pressure of the Spirit the moment he bubbles up in us and tries to win us over and take us in tow. Ultimately all our attempts at prayer and all our methods must come to a dead end and wither away in order that the Spirit of Jesus may facilitate and validate his own prayer in our heart.

Prayer as a cry

As long as we remain in the impasse we will feel uncertainty, fear, even at times desperation. Where are we? Who is going to rescue us? Spontaneously a cry for help wells up in us: 'Out of the depths I cry to you, O Lord!' (Ps. 130:1). Thus the most primitive and rudimentary form of prayer comes naturally to our lips, the cry. I want to cry out my sense of distress. But do I dare? Would it not be better for me to be strong in prayer? On the contrary. It is precisely this moment that is very important: the freedom in prayer to cry out all my neediness in the presence of God.

The ability to cry is a profoundly human reality. We all know it was the first thing we learned to do when as newborn infants we entered the world. Our lungs were still closed and upon our first contact with the outside air, free from the womb, we almost choked. At that moment we uttered a

scream. It was a life-giving scream. In the act of crying we
tore our lungs open to let the air in. It was the cry of our
beginning, the primal scream that saved us from death and
gave us life for ever.

The memory of that primal scream remains engraved on
our psyche and our body. We are marked by it for good. Each
time we find ourselves in difficult situations the echo of that
scream resurfaces. Accordingly, the capacity to scream, and
the privilege of crying out our distress, is always liberating
and in some cases the first step toward healing. A recent
psychoanalytic school has worked out this fact technically into
a therapy, primal-scream therapy. It consists in letting the
patient cry to give him or her a chance to learn to scream out
the unconscious pain that has been paralyzing him or her for
years.

One comes into the world with a cry. One also cries as one
lives, often unconsciously. Jesus even died in the midst of a
cry: 'Then Jesus, crying with a loud voice, said . . .' What he
cried out to his Father was the pain of death but also his love
and self-surrender: 'Into your hands I commend my spirit'
(Luke 23:46). His death was a cry of fear and of trust. His
death was prayer. His death was also a Pentecost, as John
suggests with the double meaning of the words: 'he gave up
the spirit'; he yielded up his spirit and at the same time passed
the Spirit on to his disciples. Jesus' death-cry is for us the
fountain of all prayer.

In the Bible as a whole – in the book of Psalms for instance
– there is a lot of crying out to God. The book of Job, in
particular, is nothing but a colossal cry of desperation and
rebellion. Job finds himself at an impasse, and no human
being, no friend, can get him out of it. He cries out in order
to bring his protests to the ear of God. Gradually it becomes
a cursing cry; he curses God who inflicted all this suffering
on him by giving him life. That is the length to which the
impasse can take us, even in prayer. We must remember,
however, that this cursing cry of Job was so genuine and so
deeply human that God had it included in the Bible he
inspired. His cursing is somehow the Word of God to us. God
knows our desperation and, as with Job, wants to hear it cried
out again and give us too a chance to join in the cry. In this

way he sympathizes with us. He waits for this cry as he also
waited for the cries of Job and the cries of his beloved Son,
Jesus Christ. For this cry and this impasse are the only way
by which he can heal and rescue us human beings.

As one delves into the ancient monastic literature, one is
struck by the fact that such cries are also the usual material
from which the first monks made up their prayer formulas.
Usually these cries were taken from the gospel: 'Have mercy
on us; Save us; Heal us; O that I might see; Be merciful to
me, a sinner.' Again what we are hearing are cries arising
from the impasse and the depths of misery.

The ability to cry out our distress is an important step. As
we do this we become familiar, little by little, with our misery.
That is a positive element. We no longer suppress our misery.
On the contrary, we identify with it so well that we can give
voice to it in cry and prayer.

Every need, pain, or desire is an extremely precious human
fact. Every desire in us is worth listening to. However strange
this may seem at first, it conceals a much deeper need that
clamours to be heard. Accordingly, every desire in us must
be listened to with attentiveness and also love. Thus, gradually, our desires must be unveiled, detached, uprooted, until
our deepest desire emerges. Because this inmost desire always
has something to do with God, this uprooting of our desires
also has always to do with the impasse of prayer. Every desire
can be heard and healed by the Word of God for which we
so intensely yearned during prayer.

The cry not only reveals my misery; it is also addressed to
someone. This too is a very fruitful aspect of prayer. When I
turn to someone I at last step outside of myself in order to
appeal to another. This is not as easy as it sounds, nor as
self-evident, especially when I am praying. Only a situation
of deep distress will force a person to come out of his shell
and to cry out to another.

This does not always happen as we pray. We may be
turning over thoughts, even edifying ones – and there are
plenty of ways of thinking about God. We may be dealing
with our feelings, good intentions, plans for holiness or for
service to others. Still, at bottom, we are dealing with ourselves, our feelings, our plans. Only the scream opens me up

at a deeper level. It is an important step in the right direction
– even if the Other seems absent, and I keep groping in the
dark. I still know that he listens to me and I trust he will
answer me. I do not have to see him. My cry reaches him.
In a sense it is even my cry that makes him present. By way
of my crying I am no longer turned in on myself or on my
own spiritual experiences. I am now totally attuned to him –
even in the dark.

Deep within me I am *myself* the cry that needs healing, and
also the cry by which I will be healed. My cry contains the
echoes of numerous other cries. There is my own primal
scream; there are the cries of my sinfulness and impotence,
and the cries of Job and the Psalmist, and finally the cry of
Jesus' *angst* and surrender. By way of all these cries I will
penetrate to the most fundamental cry within me, the cry I
have never been able to hear well, the cry of the Holy Spirit
within me: Abba, Father! Paul says it outright: 'God has sent
the Spirit of his Son into our hearts, crying, "Abba, Father!"
(Gal. 4:6). This cry of God will increasingly and gradually
become our own. It is proof that now we are really sons* of
God. We have the right to make this cry of the Spirit our
own. Somewhere in the heart of God, among the three Persons
of the Trinity, we have the God-given privilege of stammering
along with the Son: 'Abba, Father!' What else is prayer but an
attempt to make room for and to chime in with this unceasing
murmuring of the Spirit? Happy is the person who has been
able to tune in to some of this and incorporate it in his own
prayer.

The moment we begin to overhear this, all danger of an
entanglement between God and us is for ever past. For God
is open to his entire creation. The murmuring of the Spirit in
us is also interpreted by Paul as the groaning of the whole
creation which is in labour and on the point of being reborn
and passing into the new world of the Resurrection. In prayer
we catch an echo of this universal groaning. For the Spirit
intercedes for the whole world, the material as well as the
immaterial. To pray is to allow oneself to be caught up in the

---

*I have retained the word 'sons' and refrained from replacing it with
'children' because the idea is not descent but privilege and entitlement.
Translator.

emergence of the New Creation that slowly but steadily grows toward completion in Jesus Christ. Prayer is the effervescence of this new life in us, the life of the Resurrection. To pray is to pine unceasingly for this coming and this breakthrough: *Usquequo Domine?* How long, O Lord? *Marana tha!* Come, Lord Jesus!

The best prayer cry is, accordingly, the name of Jesus, the name that is simultaneously the summary *par excellence* of the Word of God. At a very early stage the first monks adopted the habit of using the name of Jesus in their ejaculatory prayers: Jesus, help me! Jesus, save me! Jesus, have mercy! The medieval custom of the East – traces of which can also be found in the West – of adding the name of Jesus to the prayer of the publican, is sufficiently well known and has again found wide acceptance today: 'Lord Jesus, Son of God, be merciful to me, a sinner.' This cry arises from our deepest distress, from the growing awareness of the sin that turns us away from true love. In any case, no prayer is possible for a Christian unless it arises from the awareness that he is a sinner – an awareness that only God can give him, at that moment in which he forgives the sin and accepts him back in love. Accordingly, the Jesus prayer is not only a first step on the road of prayer; it is already a high point, a memorial of the merciful Father who ever allows us anew to fall back into his arms.

For some this love-filled repetition, the breathing-in-and-out of Jesus' name, will be amply sufficient. For them the name that is above every name, God's first name, expresses all sorts of feelings – repentance as well as love, confession of guilt as well as the most intimate union. In the end the name of Jesus becomes a soft murmur that, little by little, drowns out all the other sounds of the heart. In time the soul of prayer will pitch its tent in it. It makes its home in the Name; it lives in the Love, sitting on the rim of the well in the depths of the heart, depths which open up in God. Eventually repetition of the name Jesus takes on a dizzying quality. But the dizziness is no one other than God himself, secretly living in our heart. We need then only yield a little to that dizziness in order to fall back continually in God.

Thus prayer takes us into the inmost core of our being. It

unifies us. It delivers us up to Jesus, but at the same time restores our own, true identify. As we repeat the name of Jesus we get to know our own name, the name he alone knòws and ever tries to teach us. As in the night we attempt to recognize the features of his face, we again find our own. And as we delivèr ourselves up to his Love, we ourselves at last learn to love – and for good.

Integration from the inside out

From the moment we have found the deep core of our being as we prayed, we will attempt to live from within that core. For a long time, like Saint Augustine, we sought God outside ourselves, but in vain. Now we know from experience that he is within, closer to me than my inmost self (*intimior intimo meo*). He is our primal ground, the hidden side of ourselves. His life bubbles up from within us. Jesus comes out to meet us from the inside (Ruysbroek). For this reason we must look for him there, on the inside. Then, turned and directed inward, we must wait for him there. We will learn to live inwardly, to be *turned inward*. Yet the moment we have built that bridge to the interior we will quickly notice that this reality in our inmost being is not only the core and point of gravity but also the wellspring from which our whole being will be restructured – the fountain of power, light, and life. It is all given to us from within us, and all our faculties will function well only to the degree they are connected with this inner world. The new 'man' is fructified from within just as he is also led by the Spirit from within.

To describe this process of simplifying and restructuring, the Byzantine tradition possesses a colourful expression; it says the mind (the *nous*) descends into the heart. This means that the mind temporarily abandons its independent abstract explorations in order first to arrive at union with the heart where the affective and intuitive faculties are hidden. Such a union of mind and heart, even at a purely natural level, leads a person to profound serenity.

But there is more. As we saw earlier, the heart is also the place where God is present in humankind. There a person can, as it were, touch the being of God and connect with him.

The idea of the mind descending into the heart then means that the whole being is taken up into the life of God, into the working of the Holy Spirit who thus becomes the unifying, integrating factor of being as a whole. At that point a person will recover all their faculties, without exception. We referred above to a kind of fast, the disengagement of the faculties. This was only temporary. For ultimately, no part of our humanity will be lost in prayer. On the contrary. Now the mind may, with impunity, lean on the heart because the heart has been completely won over by the ardour of the Spirit and has rediscovered its depth, its prayer-base. In this way the mind has again found its link with prayer. By prayer, and at the same time by love, the mind is illumined from within. It gains new and unalloyed insight because it is fructified by love.

From this point on loving can no longer occur without knowing, or knowing without loving. Loving as such has now become knowing. Love is the source of all genuine, deep knowledge. Now the famous formula, recurrent in the mystical literature of the West since Gregory the Great, has become reality: Love itself has become knowledge (*Ipse amor notitia est*). Not that it has taken the place of the intellect but it has set the intellect aglow from within, as fire smoulders beneath ash.

What is true of the mind or intellect now applies also to all our other faculties, particularly to our affective relationship to our fellow humans. All of life is now sustained by this new reality, the reality freed by prayer in the depths of our being. Prayer has become the warm, constant undertone, the musical background, against which our active daily life can continue as intensely as before. It can be still more intense and more effective because we have at last discovered the true source of our being and will only work from within it. It is an undertone that cannot hinder or disturb anyone or anything but rather creates a climate we can no longer do without. It is *dulcis memoria*, as the ancient writers called it, a sweet and luxuriant remembering of the Well-beloved that always and everywhere pervades our experiences and drowns out all other sounds.

Freedom in the Spirit

Someone who perfectly experiences the love of another can become completely free. Genuine freedom is the active reflection of God's love within a human person. When prayer has become nothing other than the increasing awareness of the life of God in us, it will have its roots very close to the source of our freedom. The experience of prayer then becomes, on a daily basis, the determining norm of our speaking and acting, the spiritual Law that inspires and animates us from within. We now carry with us, as it were, an ardour whose warmth we can pass on to others.

This process of learning to act from the inside outward signals a very important change in the life of a believing person. Up to now he had accomplished a great deal. As a rule he had acted from a kind of spontaneous and natural magnanimity. He experienced, however, that such magnanimity does not go far and soon shows signs of exhaustion. In other people an innate sense of duty plays an important role. This sense of duty, in which moral precept is the predominant factor, calls for precise analysis. What actually happens in me when I alone try energetically to be a conscientious human being? We know from experience that in the long run this can become intolerable. The danger is that it causes people to grow awry, or even become truncated, and blocks the flow of genuine life.

Someone who is given the ability to listen to his heart, however, is also at the same time sensitized to the gentle propulsion of the Holy Spirit in him. Unseen and often unfelt, the Spirit urges and prompts us onward. It has to become in each of us an internal guide. Someone who is thus led by the Spirit begins to feel instinctively, not what is best or most virtuous as such, but only that to which he is firmly driven by the Spirit, that which the Spirit asks of him at the moment – nothing more, nothing less. He can respond to the Spirit. He lives his life easily and relaxedly on this internal wavelength, able to catch the signals of the Spirit.

Saint Augustine calls it the voice of the 'internal Teacher' (*Magister interior*). We here recognize the interior anointing which John mentions in his first letter, the anointing no believer lacks:

> You have received the anointing of the Holy One and all of you are full of knowledge . . . I write these things to you concerning those who would deceive you. As for you, the anointing that you received from him abides in you and so you do not need anyone to teach you. As this anointing teaches you about all things, and is true and is not a lie, and just as it has taught you, abide in him. (1 John 2:20, 26–7)*

---

*Translated from the Dutch version used by the author.

POSTSCRIPT

When believing fifteenth- and sixteenth-century artists wanted to convey an idea of committed faith, they usually referred to a remarkable event in the life of Saint Jerome. Most museums in Flanders, and some churches, have preserved records of it. We want to conclude with this story, for it speaks with exceptional clarity to the issues we have discussed.

Long before he became a learned and famous Bible scholar and flourished on the Aventine in Rome as the spiritual leader of a group of high-society ladies, Jerome had first tried to live the life of a hermit in one of the wadis of the Judean desert, a wadi known even then for its grottoes and caves. This experience was not, however, what he had expected. With the somewhat reckless over-confidence of his age the young Jerome had diligently devoted himself to the many forms of ascesis then practised by the monks. The benefits, however, escaped him. Time would soon show that his true calling lay elsewhere in the Church and that his stay among the monks in Palestine would be merely the prelude to this.

Jerome still had much to learn, for as a young novice he was hopelessly stuck. Despite all his noble efforts, no answering voice came to him from heaven. He drifted directionless on the troubled waters of his mind, so that long-familiar temptations again began to creep up on him incessantly. Jerome lost his courage. Where had he erred? Where lay the cause of this breakdown in his relationship with God? And how could he again tune in to the wavelength of grace?

So Jerome worried and brooded, until suddenly he glimpsed a crucifix that had positioned itself between the dry branches of a dead tree. He threw himself on the ground, beating his breast with firm, sweeping movements. It is in that humble, but at the same time insistent, posture that most painters depict him.

It was not long before Jesus broke the silence and addressed Jerome from the cross.

'Jerome,' said he, 'what do you have to give me? What am I getting from you?'

That voice alone put fresh heart into Jerome again and he immediately began to wonder what he could offer his crucified friend.

'The loneliness, Lord,' he answered. 'I offer to you the loneliness with which I am struggling.'

'Excellent, Jerome,' replied Jesus, 'and thank you very much. You have certainly done your best. But have you anything more to give me?'

Not for a minute did Jerome doubt that he had much more to offer Jesus.

'Of course, Lord,' he resumed. 'My fasting, my hunger and thirst. I only eat after sundown!'

Again Jesus answered: 'Excellent, Jerome, and thank you very much. I know it. You have really done your best. But have you anything else to give me?'

Again Jerome reflected on what he might be able to give Jesus. Successively he trotted out his vigils, his long psalmody, his study of the Bible night and day, the celibacy to which he devoted himself as best he could, the lack of conveniences, the poverty, the most unexpected guests he tried to welcome without grumbling and with a not too unfriendly face, and finally the heat of the day and the chill of the night.

Each time Jesus congratulated and thanked him. He had known for a long time that Jerome meant very well.

But with a half-smile on his lips, he also persisted with his questions, asking for more: 'Jerome, is there nothing else you can give me? Or is this all?'

At long last Jerome had summed up all the good things he was able to scrape together from his memory. So when Jesus asked the question one more time he had no choice but, in great perplexity and almost total defeat to protest: 'But, Lord, have I not given you everything? I have nothing further to offer.'

Then Jesus replied – and it became deathly quiet in the hermitage and in the whole Judean wilderness – and said: 'But you do, Jerome. You have forgotten something: you must also give me your sins, that I may forgive them.'

CISTERCIAN PUBLICATIONS, INC.
TITLES LISTING

—CISTERCIAN TEXTS—

THE WORKS OF BERNARD OF CLAIRVAUX

Apologia to Abbot William
Five Books on Consideration: Advice to a Pope
Homilies in Praise of the Blessed Virgin Mary
The Life and Death of Saint Malachy the Irishman
Love without Measure: Extracts from the Writings of St Bernard (Paul Dimier)
On Grace and Free Choice
On Loving God (Analysis by Emero Stiegman)
The Parables of Saint Bernard (Michael Casey)
Sermons for the Summer Season
Sermons on Conversion
Sermons on the Song of Songs I–IV
The Steps of Humility and Pride

THE WORKS OF WILLIAM OF SAINT THIERRY

The Enigma of Faith
Exposition on the Epistle to the Romans
Exposition on the Song of Songs
The Golden Epistle
The Mirror of Faith
The Nature of Dignity of Love
On Contemplating God, Prayer & Meditations

THE WORKS OF AELRED OF RIEVAULX

Dialogue on the Soul
Liturgical Sermons, I
The Mirror of Charity
Spiritual Friendship
Treatises I: On Jesus at the Age of Twelve, Rule for a Recluse, The Pastoral Prayer
Walter Daniel: The Life of Aelred of Rievaulx

THE WORKS OF JOHN OF FORD

Sermons on the Final Verses of the Songs of Songs I–VII

THE WORKS OF GILBERT OF HOYLAND

Sermons on the Songs of Songs I–III
Treatises, Sermons and Epistles

OTHER EARLY CISTERCIAN WRITERS

The Letters of Adam of Perseigne I
Alan of Lille: The Art of Preaching
Baldwin of Ford: Spiritual Tractates I–II
Gertrud the Great of Helfta: Spiritual Exercises
Gertrud the Great of Helfta: The Herald of God's Loving-Kindness
Guerric of Igny: Liturgical Sermons I–[II]
Idung of Prüfening: Cistercians and Cluniacs: The Case of Cîteaux
Isaac of Stella: Sermons on the Christian Year, I–[II]
The Life of Beatrice of Nazareth
Serlo of Wilton & Serlo of Savigny: Works
Stephen of Lexington: Letters from Ireland
Stephen of Sawley: Treatises

—MONASTIC TEXTS—

EASTERN CHRISTIAN TRADITION

Besa: The Life of Shenoute
Cyril of Scythopolis: Lives of the Monks of Palestine
Dorotheos of Gaza: Discourses and Sayings
Evagrius Ponticus: Praktikos and Chapters on Prayer
Handmaids of the Lord: The Lives of Holy Women in Late Antiquity & the Early Middle Ages (Joan Petersen)
The Harlots of the Desert (Benedicta Ward)
John Moschos: The Spiritual Meadow
The Lives of the Desert Fathers
The Lives of Simeon Stylites (Robert Doran)
The Luminous Eye (Sebastian Brock)
Mena of Nikiou: Isaac of Alexandra & St Macrobius
Pachomian Koinonia I–III (Armand Vielleux)
Paphnutius: A Histories of the Monks of Upper Egypt
The Sayings of the Desert Fathers (Benedicta Ward)
Spiritual Direction in the Early Christian East (Irénée Hausherr)
Spiritually Beneficial Tales of Paul, Bishop of Monembasia (John Wortley)
Symeon the New Theologian: The Theological and Practical Treatises & The Three Theological Discourses (Paul McGuckin)
Theodoret of Cyrrhus: A History of the Monks of Syria
The Syriac Fathers on Prayer and the Spiritual Life (Sebastian Brock)

CISTERCIAN PUBLICATIONS, INC.
TITLES LISTING

WESTERN CHRISTIAN TRADITION

Anselm of Canterbury: Letters I–III (Walter Fröhlich)
Bede: Commentary on the Acts of the Apostles
Bede: Commentary on the Seven Catholic Epistles
Bede: Homilies on the Gospels III
The Celtic Monk (U. O Maidín)
Gregory the Great: Forty Gospel Homilies
The Meditations of Guigo I, Prior of the Charterhouse (A. Gordon Mursell)
Peter of Celle: Selected Works
The Letters of Armand-Jean de Rancé I–II
The Rule of the Master
The Rule of Saint Augustine
The Wound of Love: A Carthusian Miscellany

CHRISTIAN SPIRITUALITY

Abba: Guides to Wholeness & Holiness East & West
A Cloud of Witnesses: The Development of Christian Doctrine (David N. Bell)
The Call of Wild Geese (Matthew Kelty)
Cistercian Way (André Louf)
The Contemplative Path
Drinking From the Hidden Fountain (Thomas Spidlík)
Eros and Allegory: Medieval Exegesis of the Song of Songs (Denys Turner)
Fathers Talking (Aelred Squire)
Friendship and Community (Brian McGuire)
From Cloister to Classroom
The Silent Herald of Unity: The Life of Maria Gabrielle Sagheddu (Martha Driscoll)
Life of St Mary Magdalene and of Her Sister St Martha (David Mycoff)
Many Mansions (David N. Bell)
The Name of Jesus (Irénée Hausherr)
No Moment Too Small (Norvene Vest)
Penthos: The Doctrine of Compunction in the Christian East (Irénée Hausherr)
Rancé and the Trappist Legacy (A.J. Krailsheimer)
The Roots of the Modern Christian Tradition
Russian Mystics (Sergius Bolshakoff)
Sermons in A Monastery (Matthew Kelty)
The Spirituality of the Christian East (Tomas Spidlík)
The Spirituality of the Medieval West (André Vauchez)
Tuning In To Grace (André Louf)
Wholly Animals: A Book of Beastly Tales (David N. Bell)

—MONASTIC STUDIES—

Community and Abbot in the Rule of St Benedict I–II (Adalbert De Vogüé)
The Finances of the Cistercian Order in the Fourteenth Century (Peter King)
Fountains Abbey & Its Benefactors (Joan Wardrop)
The Hermit Monks of Grandmont (Carole A. Hutchison)
In the Unity of the Holy Spirit (Sighard Kleiner)
The Joy of Learning & the Love of God: Essays in Honor of Jean Leclercq
Monastic Practices (Charles Cummings)
The Occupation of Celtic Sites in Ireland by the Canons Regular of St Augustine and the Cistercians (Geraldine Carville)
Reading Saint Benedict (Adalbert de Vogüé)
The Rule of St Benedict: A Doctrinal and Spiritual Commentary (Adalbert de Vogüé)
The Rule of St Benedict (Br. Pinocchio)
Serving God First (Sighard Kleiner)
St Hugh of Lincoln (David H. Farmer)
Stones Laid Before the Lord (Anselme Dimier)
What Nuns Read (David N. Bell)
With Greater Liberty: A Short History of Christian Monasticism & Religious Orders (Karl Frank)

—CISTERCIAN STUDIES—

Aelred of Rievaulx: A Study (Aelred Squire)
Athirst for God: Spiritual Desire in Bernard of Clairvaux's Sermons on the Song of Songs (Michael Casey)
Beatrice of Nazareth in Her Context (Roger De Ganck)
Bernard of Clairvaux & the Cistercian Spirit (Jean Leclercq)
Bernard of Clairvaux: Man, Monk, Mystic (Michael Casey) Tapes and readings
Bernard of Clairvaux: Studies Presented to Dom Jean Leclercq
Bernardus Magister (Nonacentenary)
Christ the Way: The Christology of Guerric of Igny (John Morson)
Cistercian Sign Language (Robert Barakat)
The Cistercian Spirit
The Cistercians in Denmark (Brian McGuire)
The Cistercians in Scandinavia (James France)
A Difficult Saint (Brian McGuire)
The Eleventh-century Background of Cîteaux (Bede K. Lackner)

CISTERCIAN PUBLICATIONS, INC.

TITLES LISTING

A Gathering of Friends: Learning &
Spirituality in John of Forde (Costello
and Holdsworth)
Image and Likeness: The Augustinian
Spirituality of William of St Thierry
(David N. Bell)
An Index of Authors & Works in Cistercian
Libraries in Great Britain I (David N.
Bell)
The Mystical Theology of St Bernard
(Etiénne Gilson)
Nicolas Cotheret's Annals of Cîteaux (Louis
J. Lekai)
A Second Look at Saint Bernard (Jean
Leclercq)
The Spiritual Teachings of St Bernard of
Clairvaux (John R. Sommerfeldt)
Studiosorum Speculum (Louis J. Lekai)
Towards Unification with God (Beatrice of
Nazareth in Her Context, 2)
William, Abbot of St Thierry
Women and St Bernard of Clairvaux
(Jean Leclercq)

MEDIEVAL RELIGIOUS —WOMEN—

Lillian Thomas Shank and John A. Nichols, editors
Distant Echoes
Peace Weavers
Hidden Springs: Cistercian Monastic
Women (2 volumes)

–CARTHUSIAN TRADITION–

The Call of Silent Love
Guigo II: The Ladder of Monks & Twelve
Meditations (Colledge & Walsh)
Interior Prayer (A Carthusian)
Meditations of Guigo II (A. Gorden Mursell)
The Way of Silent Love (A Carthusian
Miscellany)
The Wound of Love (A Carthusian
Miscellany)
They Speak by Silences (A Carthusian)
Where Silence is Prayer (A Carthusian)

–STUDIES IN CISTERCIAN– ART & ARCHITECTURE

Meredith Parsons Lillich, editor
Volumes II, III and IV are now available

—THOMAS MERTON—

The Climate of Monastic Prayer (T. Merton)
The Legacy of Thomas Merton (P. Hart)
The Message of Thomas Merton (P. Hart)
The Monastic Journey of Thomas Merton
(P. Hart)

Thomas Merton Monk & Artist (Victor
Kramer)
Thomas Merton on St Bernard
Toward an Integrated Humanity
(M. Basil Pennington ed.)

CISTERCIAN LITURGICAL —DOCUMENTS SERIES—

Chrysogonus Waddell, ocso, editor
Hymn Collection of the Abbey of the
Paraclete
Institutiones nostrae: The Paraclete Statutes
Molesme Summer-Season Breviary (4
volumes)
Old French Ordinary & Breviary of the
Abbey of the Paraclete: Text &
Commentary (2 volumes)
The Cadouin Breviary (2 volumes)
The Twelfth-century Cistercian Hymnal
(2 volumes)
The Twelfth-century Cistercian Psalter
The Twelfth-century Usages of the
Cistercian Lay brothers
Two Early *Libelli Missarum*

–STUDIA PATRISTICA XVIII–

Volumes 1, 2 and 3

❖❖❖❖❖❖❖❖❖❖❖❖❖

*Editorial queries & advance book information
should be directed to the Editorial Offices:*

CISTERCIAN PUBLICATIONS
Institute of Cistercian Studies
WMU Station
Kalamazoo, Michigan 49008
Tel: (616) 387-8920 ❖ Fax: (616) 387-8921
Cistercian Publications is a non-profit
corporation. Its publishing program is
restricted to monastic texts in translation
and books on the monastic tradition.

*North American customers may order these
books through booksellers or directly from
the warehouse at:*

CISTERCIAN PUBLICATIONS
St Joseph's Abbey
Spencer, Massachusetts 01562-1233
Tel: (508) 885-8730 ❖ Fax: (508) 885-4687

British & European Orders:

CISTERCIAN PUBLICATIONS
Mount Saint Bernard Abbey
Coalville, Leicester LE67 5UL
Fax: [44] (1530) 81.46.08

❖❖❖❖❖❖❖❖❖❖❖❖❖

*A complete catalogue of texts in translation
and studies on early, medieval, and modern
monasticism is available, free of charge, from
Cistercian Publications.*

LaVergne, TN USA
24 August 2009
155701LV00002B/2/P